# THE HARTLEY AP
# HISTORY STUDY GUIDE 2024

Everything You Need to Know to Ace SAQ, DBQ & LEQ, Get an A in
Your Class and Score a 5 on The APUSH Exam Day

By

**The Hartley Publishing**

# COPYRIGHT AND DISCLAIMER

# TABLE OF CONTENTS

**INTRODUCTION** ...................................................................................... 1

**EXAM FORMAT AND STRUCTURE** ................................................3

*Section I (Multiple Choice and Short Answer)* .................................3

Part A: Multiple Choice and Short Answer .................................3

Scoring for Section I – Part A: Multiple Choice ...................5

Part B: Short-Answer Questions (SAQ) ...................................... 6

Scoring for Section I – Part B: Short Answer ........................7

*Section II* ............................................................................................... 8

1. Document-Based Question ........................................................ 8

Skills Assessed in the DBQ ...................................................... 9

Scoring on DBQ ........................................................................ 11

2. Long Essay Question ................................................................13

Scoring on LEQ ........................................................................14

**STRATEGIES FOR ANSWERING THE MULTIPLE-CHOICE QUESTIONS** ...17

1. Read the Questions Carefully ................................................ 17

2. Use Process of Elimination ....................................................18

3. Make Educated Guesses .........................................................19

4. Manage Your Time Wisely ..................................................... 20

5. Don't Leave Any Unanswered Questions ............................. 22

6. Stay Calm and Confident .......................................................23

*SAMPLE MULTIPLE-CHOICE QUESTIONS AND ANSWER* .................... 24

**MASTERING THE SAQ (SHORT ANSWER QUESTION)** ........................ 41

*1. Answering the Prompt* ...........................................................41

*2. Provide Evidence* ................................................................... 42

*3. Structure Your Response* ...................................................... 44

*SAMPLE QUESTIONS AND MODEL ANSWERS* .................................47

**EXCELLING IN THE DBQ (DOCUMENT-BASED QUESTION)** ................50

*1. Analyze the Documents* ......................................................... 50

*2. Craft a Thesis* ...................................................................................*50*

*3. Develop an Argument* ..........................................................................*51*

*4. Use Evidence from the Documents* .........................................................*51*

*5. Incorporate Outside Knowledge* ............................................................*51*

*6. Write a Strong Introduction* ..................................................................*52*

*7. Write Well-Structured Body Paragraphs* ..............................................*52*

*8. Write a Compelling Conclusion* .............................................................*53*

*SAMPLE QUESTIONS AND MODEL ESSAY* ...............................................*55*

**TACKLING THE LEQ (LONG ESSAY QUESTION)** .......................... **60**

*1. Choose the Option You're Most Comfortable With* .................................*60*

*2. Time Management* .................................................................................*60*

*3. Brainstorm and Outline* ........................................................................*60*

*4. Write a Strong Thesis Statement* ..........................................................*61*

*5. Use Evidence and Analysis Effectively* ..................................................*61*

*6. Maintain a Clear Structure and Organization* .......................................*62*

*7. Review and Revise Your Essay* ..............................................................*65*

*SAMPLE LEQs AND MODEL ESSAYS* ......................................................*66*

**COMPREHENSIVE CONTENT REVIEW** ...................................... **71**

*Period 1: Colonial America (1491-1754)* ..................................................*71*

*Period 2: The Revolutionary Era (1754-1783)* ..........................................*73*

*Period 3: The New Nation (1783-1820)* .....................................................*75*

*Period 4: The Age of Expansion and Reform (1820-1860)* .........................*77*

*Period 5: The Era of Civil War and Reconstruction (1860-1877)* ..............*79*

*Period 6: Industrialization and the Growth of the West (1865-1898)* .......*80*

*Period 7: The Emergence of Modern America (1890-1945)* ........................*83*

*Period 8: Cold War and Civil Rights Era (1945-1980)* ..............................*84*

*Period 9: Post-Cold War and Twenty-First Century America (1980-Present)* .........*86*

**EFFECTIVE STUDY TECHNIQUES AND TOOLS** .......................... **88**

*1. Utilize Flashcards, Mnemonics, and Other Memory Aids* ......................*88*

*2. Creating a Study Plan and Schedule* .....................................................*89*

*3. Prepare Mentally and Physically for the Exam* ....................................................... *91*

    Mental Preparation ....................................................................................... 92

        Breathing Techniques................................................................................. 92

    Physical Preparation: ................................................................................... 93

**CONCLUSION** ................................................................................................ **95**

**RESOURCES AND TOOLS** ........................................................................ **97**

# INTRODUCTION

Venturing into the endeavor of comprehending the expansive realm of U.S. history, ranging from the colonial era to the contemporary era, can be an overwhelming feat, even for the most dedicated scholars. The AP U.S. History exam, in particular, poses a formidable test, requiring a deep grasp of historical occurrences, themes, and ideas, accompanied by finely honed critical thinking abilities and analytical aptitude. You can conquer this exam and achieve your academic goals with proper preparation, effective study strategies, and unyielding determination.

The Hartley AP U.S. History Study Guide 2024 is your compassionate companion in your quest to ace the APUSH exam. This meticulously curated guide offers you a wealth of indispensable resources, unit-specific study guides, comprehensive review materials, and tailored test-taking strategies. Meticulously developed by a dedicated team of educators, historians, and test-prep experts, this comprehensive study guide embodies their collective passion and expertise in writing, publishing, and teaching. Its purpose is to optimize your exam preparation journey by providing a streamlined and efficient approach.

Through the utilization of this study guide, you will unlock a meticulously tailored study plan that caters to your specific requirements. Furthermore, our strategies are thoughtfully designed to save you time, enabling you to maximize the value of your limited schedule. Furthermore, detailed explanations of question types and formats will ensure that you have a thorough understanding of the examination's requirements. Our meticulously designed practice questions, prompts, and sample essays have been developed with the understanding that every student learns differently, and they are tailored to reflect the rigor and expectations of the APUSH exam. We have incorporated key terms, a timeline of significant events, and carefully curated primary source documents to help you develop a deeper connection with the historical context and improve your ability to analyze primary and secondary sources.

We recognize the obstacles and pressures students encounter while preparing for the AP U.S. History exam but rest assured, the effectiveness of this study guide is evidenced by the achievements of our previous students, who have utilized our methods to secure top scores on the AP U.S. History exam and excel in their coursework. Under our guidance, you, too, can attain this level of success, surpass your own expectations, and unlock your true academic potential.

Are you ready to seize control of your exam preparation, embrace the challenge, and make history with The AP U.S. History Study Guide 2024? Embark on this exciting and rewarding expedition into the depths of American history, where we will stand beside you, providing the necessary comprehension and assistance at every step. Collectively, we can aid you in attaining your scholarly ambitions and overcoming any obstacles that may emerge during this voyage.

# EXAM FORMAT AND STRUCTURE

The fundamental aim of the U.S. History Exam, known as the Advanced Placement (AP) Exam, entails a meticulous assessment of students' comprehension of U.S. history concepts, events, and analytical proficiencies. This comprehensive appraisal entails a time span of 3 hours and 15 minutes, incorporating two principal sections, each consisting of two components. Multiple Choice and Short Answer questions, and Section II, which comprises Document-Based and Long Essay questions.

## Section I (Multiple Choice and Short Answer)

## Part A: Multiple Choice and Short Answer

In the AP U.S. History Exam, Section I – Part A consists of 55 multiple-choice questions that you must answer within 55 minutes. This section accounts for 40% of your total exam score. The multiple-choice questions are designed to assess your understanding of historical events and concepts and your ability to analyze various sources, interpretations, and evidence.

**The questions come in different formats, each designed to evaluate a specific skill or aspect of historical analysis.**

**Let's explore these types of questions in more detail:**

### 1. Direct Questions

These questions test your knowledge of U.S. history, focusing on key events, figures, and concepts. You might be asked to identify significant moments in American history, the contributions of notable individuals, or the principles underlying important historical documents. Direct questions are straightforward and require you to recall information you have studied in your AP U.S. History course. To answer these questions, you need a solid foundation in American history and familiarity with important terms, names, and dates.

### 2. Source-based Questions

Source-based questions challenge you to analyze primary or secondary sources and answer questions based on your understanding of these materials. Primary sources pertain to authentic documents or objects that are from the era being investigated, while secondary sources consist of evaluations, explanations, or collations produced by scholars or other professionals. Source-based questions may ask you to examine excerpts from speeches, letters, newspaper articles, photographs, maps, graphs, or other visual materials and then draw conclusions or make inferences based on your analysis of these sources. To tackle source-based questions, you must be able to comprehend and evaluate the content, context, and perspective of the source and recognize any biases or limitations that may influence the information presented.

## 3. Comparison Questions

Comparison questions require comparing and contrasting different events, historical figures, concepts, or time periods. Your capacity to scrutinize resemblances and disparities in the political, social, or economic systems of the two regions, along with the objectives and tactics employed by diverse leaders, or the repercussions of distinct policies or movements on American society might be assessed. These inquiries evaluate your aptitude to recognize patterns and correlations among seemingly unrelated historical occurrences, as well as your comprehension of the wider historical backdrop. To effectively address comparative questions, it is essential to be well-acquainted with significant themes and trends in U.S. history and be capable of drawing upon your knowledge of specific events or advancements to bolster your analysis.

## 4. Cause and Effect Questions

Cause and effect questions ask you to identify the causes or consequences of historical events or developments. You might be asked to explain the factors that led to a particular conflict, the outcomes of a specific policy or law, or the reasons for the rise or decline of a social movement. Your proficiency is assessed through these inquiries, evaluating your capacity to identify and evaluate intricate connections between numerous historical elements and the events they impacted. To effectively respond to cause and effect inquiries, you must exhibit critical thinking skills regarding the interplay among different facets of American history. This includes considering political, social, economic, and cultural forces, and comprehending how they influenced historical occurrences and advancements.

## 5. Continuity and Change Questions

Continuity and change questions require you to analyze historical patterns and trends and identify and explain changes and continuities over time. You could be asked to evaluate the degree to which a particular event or development marked a turning point in American history. These questions serve as a measure of your capacity to trace and analyze historical advancements throughout time, while also discerning the importance of both continuity and change in shaping the nation's history. In order to respond to questions about continuity and change, it is essential to possess knowledge about the wider historical backdrop and possess the ability to integrate information from various time periods, sources, and viewpoints.

## Scoring for Section I – Part A: Multiple Choice

The evaluation relies on your ability to provide the accurate answers for the multiple-choice questions, determining your score based on the total number of correct responses. To establish the raw score, the College Board employs a technique known as equating, which computes the overall count of correctly answered questions. Equating ensures that the varying difficulty of different test versions is accounted for, allowing for fair comparisons between students who took different versions of the exam. The equating process adjusts the raw scores to convert them into a comparable scale score.

The scoring range for the multiple-choice section of the AP US History Exam is 1 to 5, with the top score being 5. The scale scores are based on the percentage of questions answered correctly, and the percentage required to achieve a particular scaled score may vary slightly between exams due to the equating process.

## To calculate the final score for Section I - Part A:

*The raw score is converted into a weighted score, which takes into account the relative importance of the multiple-choice section in the overall exam. As mentioned earlier, the multiple-choice section contributes 40% to your total exam score. Therefore, your weighted Section I - Part A score will be calculated by multiplying your raw score by 0.40.*

To exemplify, assuming you responded accurately to 40 out of 55 questions, your raw score would stand at 40. To derive your weighted score, simply multiply your raw score by 0.40 (40 x 0.40 = 16). This means your weighted score for Section I - Part A would be 16.

## Part B: Short-Answer Questions (SAQ)

The short answer questions (SAQs) are designed to evaluate your ability to engage with historical material, including texts, images, graphs, and maps. Your comprehension of the content, critical thinking abilities, and proficiency in synthesizing historical evidence are put to the test through these short answer questions (SAQs). The structure of SAQs is intentionally designed to offer various avenues for you to showcase your knowledge, making it an indispensable component of the AP U.S. History Exam.

Typically, each SAQ consists of a prompt followed by multiple labeled parts (a), (b), (c), etc. The prompt can take the form of a statement or question, and each part necessitates concise and specific responses that address the requirements outlined. This format enables you to demonstrate your understanding and expertise in different facets of U.S. history within a single question. It demands analysis, evaluation, and synthesis of historical evidence and perspectives.

The prompts may require you to analyze historians' interpretations or examine historical sources, such as documents, images, graphs, or maps. On occasion, the SAQs might prompt you to draw comparisons and distinctions between varying viewpoints or eras within U.S. history. This would demand an ability to showcase comprehension of the wider historical backdrop and interrelations between those periods. Additionally, the questions might emphasize significant themes encompassing political, social, economic, or cultural advancements, thereby requiring a firm command of the historical subject matter.

In addition to the variety of content and themes, the SAQs also differ in terms of their chronological focus. The first two questions concentrate on periods 3-8, while the third question offers you a choice between two options, each covering a different set of periods. This structure allows you to choose the question that best aligns with your strengths and knowledge. Opting for Question 3 will require you to address periods 1-5, whereas Question 4 covers periods 6-10.

The format of the SAQs promotes the development of critical thinking and analytical skills. By necessitating your active participation with a wide range of historical evidence and prompting you to address multiple components within every question, you are presented with the opportunity to scrutinize, assess, and amalgamate various viewpoints and sources. This procedure entails contemplating distinct facets of U.S. history, establishing correlations between them, and showcasing your comprehension of the broader historical backdrop.

Additionally, the Short Answer Questions (SAQs) foster the development of concise and targeted responses, considering the restricted time available to address each question. This requirement helps you develop the ability to communicate complex ideas and historical analyses in a clear and efficient manner. The structure of the SAQs, with their multiple parts and varied content, requires you to demonstrate your mastery of U.S. history in a comprehensive and efficient way.

**Scoring for Section I – Part B: Short Answer**

The short answer questions (SAQs) in Section I – Part B account for 20% of your total exam score. Each of the three SAQs is graded on a scale of 0 to 3 points, making the maximum possible score for this section 9 points.

**History Exam employs a specific rubric that evaluates your responses based on the following criteria:**

**1. Thesis/Claim**

To earn a point for your thesis or claim, you must provide a clear, concise statement that directly addresses the question prompt. The thesis should demonstrate your understanding of the historical context and effectively respond to all parts of the question. An effective thesis is essential for earning full credit on the SAQs, as it sets the stage for the rest of your response.

**2. Evidence**

To earn a point for evidence, you must support your thesis with specific examples and details from your knowledge of U.S. history or from the provided sources, such as texts, images, graphs, or maps. The evidence you provide should be accurate, relevant, and sufficient to demonstrate your understanding of the historical material. Providing well-chosen evidence is crucial for earning credit on the SAQs, as it allows you to substantiate your argument and showcase your mastery of the content.

### 3. Analysis and Reasoning

To earn a point for analysis and reasoning, you must demonstrate your ability to analyze historical material, draw connections between different periods or themes, and explain the significance of your evidence. Your analysis should be logical, coherent, and insightful, showcasing your critical thinking and analytical skills. Demonstrating strong analysis and reasoning is essential for earning credit on the SAQs, as it demonstrates your ability to synthesize and interpret historical evidence effectively.

When grading your SAQs, the exam readers will apply the rubric criteria to each part of the question, awarding points based on the quality of your thesis, evidence, and analysis. It's important to note that partial credit may be awarded if your response addresses some but not all aspects of the question. To maximize your score on the SAQs, it's essential to address each part of the question and to provide a clear thesis, well-chosen evidence, and insightful analysis throughout your response.

### To calculate the weighted score for this section:

*By applying a multiplication factor of 0.2 to your raw score (the cumulative points obtained from all three questions), you can calculate your weighted score. For instance, if your total points amount to 7, your weighted score would be 7 multiplied by 0.2, resulting in 1.4.*

## Section II

### 1. Document-Based Question

The DBQ provides a set of 5 to 7 documents covering a specific topic from periods 3-10 of the AP U.S. History curriculum. The documents may include various types of materials such as written primary and secondary sources, maps, images, charts, and graphs. These documents are carefully curated to represent diverse perspectives and viewpoints related to the question prompt, allowing you to develop a nuanced and well-rounded argument.

The DBQ question prompt will typically ask you to assess a historical development or theme, compare and contrast different perspectives, or evaluate the impact of specific events or policies.

## The DBQ is structured as follows:

### 1. Reading Period

The 15-minute reading period is essential to the DBQ structure. This time is designated for you to read and analyze the documents, take notes, identify patterns or relationships between the documents, and plan your essay. During the reading period, you should also formulate a clear and concise thesis statement that responds to the question prompt and sets the direction for your essay.

### 2. Writing Period

You will have 45 minutes to write your DBQ essay following the reading period. This part of the DBQ structure allows you to demonstrate your ability to craft a well-organized, coherent essay that incorporates evidence from the documents, your knowledge of U.S. history, and your historical reasoning skills. The writing period is crucial for developing a persuasive argument and providing a detailed analysis of the documents.

### 3. Essay Structure

A successful DBQ essay should follow a clear and logical structure that includes an introduction, several body paragraphs, and a conclusion. The introduction should present your thesis statement and briefly outline your essay's main arguments. The body paragraphs should analyze the documents, use evidence to support your thesis and demonstrate your understanding of the historical context. Finally, the conclusion should synthesize your main points, restate your thesis, and leave a lasting impression on the reader.

### Skills Assessed in the DBQ

The Document-Based Question (DBQ) is designed to assess a range of historical thinking and writing skills that are essential for success in the AP U.S. History Exam.

### The key skills assessed in the DBQ include:

## 1. Thesis Development and Argumentation

Your ability to craft a clear, concise, and defensible thesis statement that directly addresses the question prompt is crucial. Developing a coherent and persuasive argument that supports your thesis requires a roadmap for your essay and setting the stage for your argument. You must utilize evidence from the documents and your own knowledge of U.S. history.

## 2. Document Analysis

The DBQ assesses your ability to analyze and interpret historical documents. This includes understanding the main ideas and arguments presented in the documents, identifying the authors' perspectives or biases, and evaluating the reliability and credibility of the sources. You must also be able to contextualize the documents within the broader historical narrative and relate them to the question prompt.

## 3. Use of Evidence

A successful DBQ essay requires you to use evidence from the documents effectively to support your argument. To fortify your argument, it is crucial to incorporate quotations or paraphrases from various documents. By doing so, you can elucidate the importance of the evidence and establish connections to your thesis. Furthermore, contrasting or corroborating evidence from different documents can enhance the strength of your argument. This comprehensive approach allows for a thorough analysis of the subject matter, providing a well-rounded and compelling case.

## 4. Contextualization

The DBQ assesses your ability to place the documents and your argument within a broader historical context. This means understanding and explaining the relevant social, political, economic, or cultural factors that influenced the events, ideas, or individuals discussed in the documents. Contextualization helps you situate your argument within the larger historical narrative and demonstrate your understanding of the forces that shaped U.S. history.

## 5. Historical Reasoning Skills

The DBQ tests your ability to employ various historical reasoning skills, such as causation, comparison, continuity and change, and periodization. Requiring your proficiency in recognizing and examining historical patterns, evaluating the importance of events or advancements, and elucidating their connections to overarching themes in the history of the United States.

## 6. Synthesis

To craft a persuasive and cohesive argument, a proficient DBQ essay should showcase your aptitude in amalgamating information extracted from the provided documents, your comprehensive understanding of U.S. history, and your adeptness in employing historical reasoning. This means bringing together multiple lines of evidence, weighing their relative importance, and drawing insightful conclusions that advance your thesis.

## 7. Writing Skills

The purpose of the DBQ is to evaluate your ability to write clearly, succinctly, and persuasively. Your essay should be well-organized, with a clear introduction, body paragraphs developing your argument, and a conclusion synthesizing your main points. Your writing should also demonstrate correct grammar, punctuation, syntax, and effective use of evidence and analysis.

## Scoring on DBQ

The Document-Based Question (DBQ) is scored on a scale of 0 to 7 points, with each point representing a specific skill or aspect of the essay. Points are allocated according to a comprehensive rubric that assesses the essay as a cohesive entity, rather than assigning grades to separate components.

## Below is a breakdown outlining the criteria for scoring:

### 1. Thesis/Claim (0-1 point)

To earn this point, your essay must have a clear and defensible thesis statement that directly addresses the question prompt and sets the stage for your argument.

## 2. Contextualization (0-1 point)

To earn this point, you must provide a broader historical context for your argument. This involves situating the documents and your argument within the larger historical narrative and explaining the relevant social, political, economic, or cultural factors that influenced the events or ideas discussed in the documents.

## 3. Evidence from the Documents (0-2 points)

To earn these points, you must effectively use evidence from the documents to support your argument. You can earn up to 2 points for using evidence from at least three documents. Connecting the evidence to your thesis necessitates incorporating quotes or paraphrases from the documents and elucidating their significance.

## 4. Evidence Beyond the Documents (0-1 point)

In order to receive this particular point, it is necessary to present supplementary proof that supports your claim, extending beyond the material covered in the provided documents. This could include historical facts, events, or developments that you have learned in your AP U.S. History course.

## 5. Analysis and Reasoning (0-2 points)

To earn these points, you must demonstrate your ability to analyze the documents and use historical reasoning skills effectively. You can earn 1 point for explaining how the documents' perspectives or historical situations relate to your argument and 1 point for employing a specific historical reasoning skill (such as causation, comparison, continuity, change, or periodization) to advance your argument.

## To calculate the weighted score for this section:

*By applying a multiplication factor of 0.25 to your raw score, you can calculate your weighted score. To illustrate, suppose you obtained 5 points on the DBQ. Multiplying this by 0.25 yields a weighted score of 1.25.*

## 2. Long Essay Question

Long Essay Question (LEQ) is designed to assess your ability to explain and analyze significant issues in U.S. history while developing a coherent argument supported by historical evidence.

When you receive the LEQ prompt, you will be given three essay choices, each focusing on the same theme and skill but in different time periods.

### The options will be divided as follows:

### Option 1: Periods 1-3

Choosing this option delves into the United States' initial chronicles, encompassing the era preceding Christopher Columbus' arrival, the existence of Native American societies, the colonial period, and concluding with the Revolutionary War. Themes of interest may encompass Native American cultures, European exploration and colonization, the dynamic exchanges between Europeans and Native Americans, the growth and structure of colonial societies, the emergence and expansion of slavery, the catalysts and ramifications of the American Revolution, and the establishment of the nascent nation. To excel in this choice, a robust comprehension of early American history is imperative, along with the ability to scrutinize pivotal events, notable figures, and influential concepts that molded the nation's progress during this momentous era.

### Option 2: Periods 4-6

Centering on the 19th century, this alternative explores the transformative epoch encompassing the early Republic, the expansion towards the west, the emergence of sectionalism, the Civil War, and the era of Reconstruction. To achieve genuine excellence in the chosen essay, a comprehensive understanding of essential themes and pivotal events of the 19th century is indispensable. These encompass, though not exclusively, the political party evolution, the profound influence of the Market Revolution, the deeply disputed and divisive discussions concerning slavery and its extension into unexplored regions, the catalysts and extensive repercussions of the Civil War, and the achievements and setbacks encountered during the era of Reconstruction. It is crucial not only to possess factual awareness of these occurrences but also the capacity to scrutinize the underlying factors and consequences of these progressions within the wider framework of American history.

## Option 3: Periods 7-10

Embarked upon the 19th-century mystic twilight, we sail on our grand voyage, venturing across the 20th-century boundless realm and reaching out into the 21st-century expansive horizons. Venturing upon the mystic twilight of the 19th century, we set sail on a grand voyage, reaching out into the expansive horizons of the 21st century. Delving into an unparalleled and extraordinary vantage point, we explore a tapestry of richly woven themes. The Civil Rights Movement, the Cold War, the Gilded Age, the Progressive Era, World Wars I and II with US involvement, and groundbreaking strides in society's politics and economics all intricately interweave in terms of exploration. The origins and aftermath of industrialization, the rise of the United States as a dominant global power, the lasting effects of influential political and social movements that have molded the current American terrain, or the clash of differing ideological viewpoints during the Cold War offer avenues for deeper investigation. Harmoniously, these elements converge when delving into the extensive tapestry of historical and societal evolution. Harmoniously,,these elements converge as we examine the intertwining of society, politics, and economics..These elements, society, politics, and economics, converge and shape the American landscape. To excel in addressing this essay prompt, a comprehensive grasp of the intricate and interwoven events and themes of the early 21st and 20th centuries is indispensable.

## Scoring on LEQ

Scoring for the Long Essay Question (LEQ) on the AP U.S. History exam is based on a rubric that assesses your ability to develop a thesis-driven argument supported by historical evidence. The LEQ is worth 15% of your total exam score.

## The rubric consists of six points, which are allocated as follows:

### 1. Thesis/Claim (0-1 point):

To earn this point, you must develop a clear and defensible thesis statement that directly addresses the question prompt and sets the stage for your argument. The thesis should provide a roadmap for your essay, outlining the main points you will use to support your argument.

### 2. Contextualization (0-1 point)

This point is awarded for providing a broader historical context relevant to the question prompt. You should demonstrate an understanding of the wider historical events, developments, or processes that are connected to the topic you are analyzing.

### 3. Evidence (0-2 points)

  a. **Evidence Beyond the Documents (0-1 points): You must support your argument with specific and relevant historical evidence that goes beyond the provided documents or sources. Some examples of supplementary materials that can be used to earn this point include further primary or secondary sources, as well as personal familiarity with the historical context.**
  b. **Evidence from the Documents (0-1 point): If the question prompt refers to specific documents or sources, you should incorporate them into your argument as evidence. You must accurately and effectively use the documents to support your thesis.**

### 4. Analysis and Reasoning (0-2 points):

  a. **Targeted Skill (0-1 point):** Each LEQ will assess a specific historical thinking skill, such as causation, comparison, or continuity, and change over time. You must clearly understand the targeted skill and apply it effectively in your analysis.
  b. **Complexity (0-1 point):** This point is awarded for demonstrating a complex understanding of the historical issue or topic. This can include recognizing and analyzing multiple perspectives, explaining the nuances of the issue, or considering the broader historical implications.

**To calculate the weighted score for this section:**

*Multiply your raw score by 0.15. For example, if you earned 4 points on the LEQ, your weighted score would be 4 * 0.15 = 0.6.*

**To calculate your total exam score, add the weighted scores from each section:**

*By amalgamating the weighted scores from distinct sections, namely Multiple Choice, Short Answer, DBQ, and LEQ, the computation of the overall exam score is ascertained. By utilizing the weighted scores of 17.6 (Multiple Choice), 1.4 (Short Answer), 1.25 (DBQ), and 0.6 (LEQ), one can derive the comprehensive exam score through the following calculation: 20.85 = 17.6 + 1.4 + 1.25 + 0.6.*

To determine the final AP score, which ranges from 1 to 5, the College Board employs distinct cutoff thresholds that are subject to annual variation, dependent on the exam's intricacy and the overall performance of examinees as a whole. Generally, a score of 3 is considered to meet the passing criteria, while achieving a score of 4 or 5 is often regarded as sufficiently high to warrant college credit or advanced placement at numerous educational institutions.

Remember, understanding how to earn points and calculate your score is essential to your AP U.S. History Exam preparation. Focusing on each section's requirements and maximizing your performance can improve your chances of achieving a high score and earning college credit.

# STRATEGIES FOR ANSWERING THE MULTIPLE-CHOICE QUESTIONS

Developing effective strategies for answering multiple-choice questions is essential when preparing for the AP US History exam.

## Here are some tips for doing well in this part:

### 1. Read the Questions Carefully

Importantly, understanding exactly what is being asked and obtaining all the important details is ensured by carefully reading questions. Misinterpreting the question can result in incorrect answers, even if you have a solid understanding of the subject matter. Thus, it is of utmost importance to closely focus on the questions to evade such pitfalls and deliver accurate responses. Even with a strong knowledge base, attentive reading and comprehension of the questions are vital to ensure that you grasp the intended meaning and provide precise answers.

### Here are some tips for carefully reading questions:

#### • Read The Entire Question

Refrain from skimming or drawing hasty conclusions based on a few keyword searches. Read the entire question to fully comprehend its context. Eliminating the desire to skip questions and maintaining concentration, for example, you would likely read "in which decade does it become increasingly popular in America?" rather than "in which decade did it become increasingly popular in America?" You could easily miss the question's context and respond, "able to read/an invention by Lewis/not many people owned slaves in the 1900s."

#### • Pay Attention to Specific Words or Phrases

To grasp the context and meaning of the question, it is crucial to closely pay attention to specific phrases and words. Seek out words that could qualify, limit, or modify the question, like "most," "least," "except," "only," or "primarily." Such words can significantly alter the question's formulation and determine the correct answer. For instance, if the question states, *"Which of the following was **NOT** a cause of the American Revolution?"* you must select the answer that doesn't align as a cause.

### • Rephrase the Question

Rephrasing the question in your own words can often enhance comprehension. By adopting this approach, you can focus your concentration on the key points and concepts embedded within the question. This approach helps remove irrelevant details and assists in pinpointing the correct answer. For instance, you can rephrase the question *"What was a significant effect of the First Great Awakening on colonial America?"* as *"How did the First Great Awakening impact colonial America?"*

Implementing these strategies ensures a comprehensive comprehension of each question, thereby minimizing the chances of providing incorrect responses. This technique will also assist you in determining how to select the most appropriate answer.

## 2. Use Process of Elimination

When faced with uncertainty about the correct response, employing the process of elimination can be helpful in narrowing down your options. Narrowing down options and making an informed choice can be effectively achieved by eliminating obviously wrong, irrelevant, or unfitting answers. This method allows for easier selection from the given options, enabling you to choose the right answer with confidence and accuracy.

**Follow this approach to streamline your decision-making process and arrive at the most suitable choice:**

### Step 1: Cross Out the Obviously Wrong Answers

Begin by eliminating options that are clearly incorrect or have no relevance to the question. The initial step of eliminating clearly incorrect, irrelevant, or misaligned options helps narrow down the available choices, enabling easier focus on the remaining options.

**For instance, let's consider the question:**

*"Which of the following was a major cause of the War of 1812?"*

## The choices are:

    **a.** The sinking of the Titanic
    **b.** British impressment of American sailors
    **c.** The Louisiana Purchase
    **d.** The invention of the cotton gin

You can immediately eliminate options A and D because they are unrelated to the War of 1812.

## Step 2: Compare and Contrast the Remaining Options

Once you've narrowed your choices, carefully compare the remaining options to determine which best answers the question. Look for any similarities or differences between the choices and consider how they relate to the question's context.

For example, with the remaining options B and C, you can compare and contrast their relevance to the War of 1812. British impressment of American sailors (option B) directly contributed to tensions between the United States and Britain. In contrast, the Louisiana Purchase (option C) was more focused on territorial expansion and had a less direct impact on the war.

Therefore, option B is the correct answer.

Doing this also allows you to be aware of any weak areas in your reasoning, which can help you confirm your answer before writing it on your test.

## 3. Make Educated Guesses

When you need help with the correct answer, make an educated guess rather than leaving the question blank. There's no penalty for guessing on the AP US History exam, so it's better to guess and potentially earn points than to leave a question unanswered.

## Here are some tips for making educated guesses:

### • Look for Patterns

The right answer may sometimes fit into a pattern with other right answers on the test. When you're not sure what to do, it might be a good strategy to choose "B" if you observe that the majority of correct answers have been "B." However, exercise caution while employing this approach since its effectiveness may vary.

### • Use Prior Knowledge

Leveraging your knowledge of US history can greatly assist in making informed guesses. Even if the answer is not entirely certain, your background knowledge enables you to eliminate improbable options and improve the likelihood of selecting the correct answer.

### • Trust Your Instincts

When guessing, trust your instincts. Consider selecting a particular answer if you have a gut feeling that it is correct. However, be sure to weigh your instincts against any evidence or reasoning that supports a different answer.

## 4. Manage Your Time Wisely

Time management is crucial during the multiple-choice section of the AP US History exam so that you have sufficient time to answer all questions and possibly review your answers.

## Here are some expanded tips on managing your time effectively:

### • Develop a System For Marking Questions

As you work through the exam, use a consistent system for marking questions that you want to skip or return to later. This can save you time when revisiting those questions. You could circle the question number, place a star next to it, or use another method that works for you.

HARTLEY PUBLISHING

## • Balance Speed And Accuracy

While it's important to maintain a steady pace, be careful to take your time with questions so quickly that you sacrifice accuracy. Take care to carefully read each question along with its available options before reaching a decision. Allocating valuable time to challenging or potentially unanswerable questions due to insufficient information is unwise. Instead, when encountering a time-consuming question, it is best to temporarily skip it and return to it later. This method becomes particularly helpful if you realize you have already spent more than five minutes on a specific question. By adopting this strategy, you can enhance your overall efficiency and boost the likelihood of providing accurate responses to a greater number of questions.

## • Regularly Check Your Progress

Taking short pauses at intervals of approximately 10 to 15 minutes proves beneficial for conducting self-evaluations. These self-checks confirm that you are making progress and following the correct path. If you identify the need for additional time to catch up, it is advisable to adjust your pace accordingly. By periodically assessing your progress, you remain mindful of your performance and can make necessary adaptations, leading to a smoother and more effective test-taking experience.

## • Review Your Answers at the End of Each Section

Upon completing each section, make it a habit to go back and thoroughly review your answers. This practice enables you to identify and rectify any careless errors or omissions before it becomes too late. It is always preferable to detect incorrect responses sooner rather than later. Moreover, the process of reviewing your answers at the end of each section allows for self-reflection, providing valuable insights into your exam preparation.

Efficient time management plays a vital role in managing stress levels and ensuring that you have ample time to respond to all the multiple-choice questions.

## 5. Don't Leave Any Unanswered Questions

On the AP US History exam, there is no penalty for guessing, so it is important to answer every question, even if you need clarification on the correct response. Leaving a blank question guarantees that you won't receive any points for that question while guessing at least gives you a chance to earn points.

In addition, it is noteworthy that there exist only a limited number of inquiries that students answer correctly or incorrectly due to mere luck. As per the College Board, the esteemed body accountable for standardized tests, it has been reported that the average probability of selecting the accurate option in a multiple-choice question is roughly 50 percent.  Guessing can be a valid strategy, particularly considering that incorrect answers are typically not penalized. Therefore, your chances of selecting the correct answer and achieving a favorable outcome in multiple-choice questions can significantly improve by considering educated guesses.

Consequently, your overall score can be positively impacted by answering every question, even if you are unsure of the correct answer.

## 6. Stay Calm and Confident

Staying calm and confident is an essential aspect of tackling the multiple-choice section of the AP US History exam. To optimize your focus on questions, effortless information recall, and decision-making, it is beneficial to maintain a state of relaxation and self-assurance.

**The following tips can assist you in staying calm and confident:**

**• Take Deep Breaths**

Engaging in deep breathing techniques during moments of stress or overwhelm in the exam can bring notable advantages to both your body and mind. Allocating a brief period to practice a few deep breaths can aid in restoring a sense of tranquility and balance. By implementing deep breathing techniques, which involve taking deep inhales, briefly holding the breath, and exhaling slowly, you can effectively relieve tension and regain concentration. This straightforward yet potent strategy offers a valuable pause and contributes to your overall well-being during the exam, ultimately boosting your performance capabilities.

## • Maintain a Positive Attitude

The impact of cultivating a positive attitude on your exam performance cannot be emphasized enough. Fostering confidence in your capabilities and reminding yourself of the hard work and preparation invested plays a pivotal role in attaining success. It is vital to steer clear of negative self-talk, redirect your attention towards your strengths, and acknowledge the knowledge you possess. By nurturing a positive mindset, you can greatly enhance your overall performance and approach the exam with optimism and self-assurance, ultimately positioning yourself for triumph.

## • Concentrate on a Single Question at a Time

Stay calm during the entire exam. To enhance your likelihood of success in the multiple-choice section of the AP US History test, it is advisable to employ a focused approach by tackling one question at a time. By treating each question as a separate challenge, you can maximize your chances of achieving a positive outcome and adequately address all the questions. Devote your full concentration to each question before proceeding to the next. Implementing these strategies will optimize your success and guarantee that you fully attend to each question, eliminating the possibility of incomplete or incorrect responses.

## SAMPLE MULTIPLE-CHOICE QUESTIONS AND ANSWER

1. Of the following, which cause was significant in the American Revolution?

      A.    The War of 1812
      B.    The Louisiana Purchase
      C.    The Stamp Act
      D.    The Emancipation Proclamation

Answer: C

2. Which U.S. President was responsible for the Louisiana Purchase in 1803?

   A.    George Washington
   B.    John Adams
   C.    Thomas Jefferson
   D.    James Madison

Answer: C

3. The January 6, 2021 attack on the U.S. Capitol was a response to:

    A.    The COVID-19 pandemic and lockdown measures
    B.    The 2020 presidential election results
    C.    Racial injustice and police violence
    D.    Gun control measures and Second Amendment rights

Answer: B

4. The term "Manifest Destiny" was used to describe what?

    A.    The belief in a strong central government
    B.    The belief in the abolition of slavery
    C.    The belief that the United States was destined to expand westward
    D.    The belief in the superiority of the American political system

Answer: C

5. The policy of containment during the Cold War was primarily aimed at:

    A.    Preventing the spread of communism
    B.    Expanding U.S. territorial possessions
    C.    Limiting the power of the United Nations
    D.    Reducing the influence of European powers in the Americas

Answer:A

6. Which of the following Supreme Court cases established the principle of judicial review?

    A.    Marbury v. Madison
    B.    Brown v. Board of Education

C. Dred Scott v. Sandford
D. Plessy v. Ferguson

Answer: A

7. The COVID-19 pandemic, which began in 2020, led to:

A. An economic recession and a surge in unemployment
B. A significant reduction in greenhouse gas emissions
C. A surge in the stock market and increased wealth inequality
D. All of the above

Answer: D

8. The impeachment of President Donald Trump in 2019 was related to:

A. Allegations of collusion with Russia in the 2016 election
B. Allegations of obstruction of justice and abuse of power
C. The handling of the COVID-19 pandemic
D. The implementation of the Affordable Care Act

Answer: B

9. What was the main purpose of the Interstate Commerce Act (1887)?

A. To regulate railroad rates and practices
B. To control the growth of monopolies and trusts
C. To improve working conditions in factories
D. To promote economic development in the Western United States

Answer: A

10. The Harlem Renaissance of the 1920s was a:

    A.    Political movement that sought to end racial segregation
    B.    African American art, music, and writing were central to a cultural movement.
    C.    Period of rapid economic growth in the United States
    D.    Social movement that sought to improve living conditions in urban areas

Answer: B

11. The primary goal of Franklin D. Roosevelt's New Deal was what?

    A.    Reform the banking system
    B.    Provide relief, recovery, and reform in response to the Great Depression
    C.    Increase U.S. involvement in world affairs
    D.    Promote labor rights and protections

Answer: B

12. Which of the following did not cause the Great Depression?

    A.    Agricultural overproduction
    B.    Stock market speculation
    C.    High levels of government spending
    D.    Bank failures and lack of credit

Answer: C

13. The policy of appeasement in the 1930s aimed at:

    A.    Stopping the spread of communism
    B.    Maintaining peace by giving in to some of Adolf Hitler's demands
    C.    Supporting European colonies in their fight for independence
    D.    Encouraging the disarmament of aggressive nations

Answer: B

14. The Truman Doctrine and the Marshall Plan were both aimed at:

A. Encouraging post-World War II economic recovery in Europe
B. Promoting democracy and containing communism
C. Reducing military spending and promoting peace
D. Encouraging the United Nations to take a more active role in world affairs

Answer: B

15. The Me Too movement that gained momentum in 2017 was primarily focused on:

A. Promoting women's rights and combating sexual harassment and assault
B. Advocating for LGBTQ+ rights and marriage equality
C. Combatting climate change and promoting sustainable practices
D. Advocating for gun control and school safety

Answer: A

16. The direct result of the Cuban Missile Crisis of 1962 was what?

A. The failed Bay of Pigs invasion
B. The United States placed nuclear missiles in Turkey
C. Soviet attempts to install nuclear missiles in Cuba
D. American efforts to overthrow Fidel Castro

Answer: C

17. The Watergate scandal ultimately led to:

A. The impeachment and removal of President Richard Nixon
B. The resignation of President Richard Nixon

C.    The impeachment and removal of President Bill Clinton
D.    The passage of significant campaign finance reform legislation


Answer: B


18. The purpose of the War Powers Resolution (1973) was to:

A.    Expand the power of the President to wage war without Congressional approval
B.    Limit the power of the President to wage war without Congressional approval
C.    Increase funding for the United States military
D.    Authorize the use of military force in Vietnam


Answer: B


19. The term "Gilded Age" characterizes a period of time in American history by what?

A.    Extreme wealth and poverty, as well as political corruption
B.    Progressive social and political reform
C.    Rapid industrialization and urbanization
D.    Both A and C


Answer: D


20. The Iran-Contra Affair involved what?

A.    In exchange for freeing American hostages, the US is secretly selling weapons to Iran.
B.    The United States supporting the overthrow of the Iranian government
C.    The United States providing military aid to Iraq during the Iran-Iraq War
D.    The United States negotiating a nuclear deal with Iran


Answer:,A

21. To justify what concept was "Manifest Destiny" used?

    A.     Abolition of slavery
    B.     The American Revolution
    C.     The westward expansion of the United States
    D.     The establishment of an American empire overseas

Answer: C

22. Who wrote the influential Common Sense pamphlet, which argued for American independence from Britain?

    A.     Thomas Jefferson
    B.     Benjamin Franklin
    C.     Thomas Paine
    D.     John Adams

Answer: C

23. The of "Reagan Revolution" characteristics the 1980s were what?

    A.     Increased government regulation of the economy
    B.     Conservative policies including tax cuts and deregulation
    C.     The expansion of social welfare programs
    D.     A focus on civil rights and social justice issues

Answer: B

24. The Truman Doctrine, announced in 1947, was significant because it:

    A.     Established the policy of containment against the spread of communism
    B.     Declared war on the Soviet Union
    C.     Provided for the creation of the United Nations

  D.  Signaled the beginning of the Cold War

Answer: A

25. The Paris Agreement, signed in 2016, aimed to:

  A.  Establish a global climate change mitigation framework
  B.  Create a new international trade agreement
  C.  Strengthen military alliances between the United States and its European allies
  D.  Address global nuclear disarmament

Answer: A

26. The Watergate scandal led to the resignation of:

  A.  President Richard Nixon
  B.  President Gerald Ford
  C.  President Jimmy Carter
  D.  President Ronald Reagan

Answer: A

27. A major consequence of the Spanish-American War was which of the following?

  A.  The United States annexed Hawaii
  B.  The United States took control of Puerto Rico, Guam, and the Philippines.
  C.  The United States declared war on Germany
  D.  The United States became involved in the Mexican Revolution

Answer: B

28. The 1964 Civil Rights Act aimed to:

    A.    End racial segregation in public places and ban employment discrimination
    B.    Give African Americans the right to vote
    C.    Implement affirmative action policies
    D.    Abolish the poll tax

Answer: A

29. The 1965 Voting Rights Act was designed to:

    A.    Give African Americans the right to vote
    B.    Eliminate voting restrictions and discriminatory practices, such as literacy tests
    C.    Implement affirmative action policies in elections
    D.    Lower the voting age to 18

Answer: B

30. The 1960s counterculture movement in the United States was characterized by:

    A.    A return to traditional values and norms
    B.    An emphasis on consumerism and material wealth
    C.    Rejection of mainstream values and norms, with a focus on peace, love, and equality
    D.    A political shift towards conservatism

Answer: C

31. The Monroe Doctrine (1823) aimed to:

    A.    Prevent European colonization and intervention in the Western Hemisphere
    B.    Promote American expansionism and Manifest Destiny
    C.    Establish a policy of isolationism
    D.    Encourage the spread of democracy in Latin America

Answer: A

32. The Dawes Act (1887) primarily sought to:

   A.   Provide compensation to Native Americans for land taken by the U.S. government
   B.   Establish reservations for Native American tribes
   C.   Encourage the assimilation of Native Americans by dividing tribal lands into individual allotments
   D.   Recognize Native American tribes as sovereign nations

Answer: C

33. In the presidential election of 1800, often referred to as the "Revolution of 1800," who were the main opponents?

   A.   Thomas Jefferson and Aaron Burr
   B.   Thomas Jefferson and John Adams
   C.   John Adams and Alexander Hamilton
   D.   Alexander Hamilton and Aaron Burr

Answer: B

34. The purpose of the Seneca Falls Convention in 1848 was what?

   A.   To promote the abolition of slavery
   B.   To fight for women's rights and suffrage
   C.   To organize opposition to the Mexican-American War
   D.   To establish a third political party

Answer: B

35. "McCarthyism" refers to:

    A.    The political philosophy of President McCarthy
    B.    The use of propaganda during the Cold War
    C.    The anti-communist hysteria and witch hunts of the 1950s
    D.    The push for civil rights legislation during the 1960s

Answer: C

36. The Missouri Compromise of 1820 was intended to:

    A.    End the importation of slaves into the United States
    B.    Preserve the balance of power between slave states and free states in the Senate
    C.    Abolish slavery in the territories acquired from Mexico in the Mexican-American War
    D.    Grant Missouri statehood as a free state

Answer: B

37. The Seneca Falls Convention in 1848 was significant because it:

    A.    Was the first women's rights convention in the United States
    B.    Marked the end of the Civil War
    C.    Marked the beginning of the American Revolution
    D.    Resulted in the ratification of the 19th Amendment, granting women the right to vote

Answer: A

38. The Wounded Knee Massacre in 1890 marked:

    A.    The beginning of the Indian Wars in the West
    B.    A major victory for Native American forces against the U.S. Army

C.     The end of the Indian Wars and the effective containment of Native Americans on reservations

D.     The start of the Ghost Dance movement among Native American tribes

Answer: C

39. What is the Treaty of Versailles often criticized for, which ended World War I?

A.     Being too lenient on Germany
B.     Causing communism to grow in Russia
C.     Imposing harsh penalties on Germany that laid the groundwork for World War II
D.     Not addressing the root causes of the war

Answer: C

40. The Strategic Arms Reduction Treaty (START) of 1991 aimed to:

A.     Limit the production and deployment of ballistic missiles
B.     Eliminate all nuclear weapons
C.     Establish a global missile defense system
D.     Reduce the number of strategic nuclear weapons held by the United States and the Soviet Union

Answer: D

41. The Brady Bill, passed in 1993, implemented:

A.     Health care reform
B.     Gun control measures
C.     Environmental protections
D.     Economic stimulus measures

Answer: B

42. Primarily focusing on the Occupy Wall Street movement, which began in 2011, involved:

    A.     Promoting environmental protection and clean energy
    B.     Addressing income inequality and corporate influence in politics
    C.     Opposing the U.S. involvement in foreign wars
    D.     Advocating for immigration reform

Answer: B

43. During which period does the term "Reconstruction" refer to, following the American Civil War?

    A.     The United States rebuilt its infrastructure and economy
    B.     The Southern states were reintegrated into the Union, and civil rights for African Americans were addressed
    C.     The United States expanded its territories in the West
    D.     The American political system was reformed

Answer: B

44. Into law, in which year was the Patient Protection and Affordable Care Act, also known as Obamacare, signed?

    A.     1996
    B.     2000
    C.     2008
    D.     2010

Answer: D

45. The Monroe Doctrine declared that:

A.  The United States would not interfere in European affairs
B.  European powers should not colonize or interfere in the affairs of nations in the Americas
C.  The United States would support any nation in the Americas that wanted to revolt against their European colonizers
D.  The United States would use military force to protect its economic interests in the Americas

Answer: B

46. Who did the GI Bill, passed in 1944, provide benefits to?

A.  Veterans of World War II
B.  Victims of the Great Depression
C.  Refugees fleeing Europe after World War II
D.  Workers displaced by automation and outsourcing

Answer: A

47. President Lyndon B. Johnson's Great Society program aimed to achieve which of the following significant goals?

A.  Promoting civil rights and fighting poverty
B.  Expanding U.S. involvement in Vietnam
C.  Deregulating industry and promoting free-market capitalism
D.  Strengthening the U.S. military

Answer: A

48. The Tet Offensive during the Vietnam War was significant because it:

A.  Marked a turning point in the war and led to increased opposition to U.S. involvement
B.  Resulted in a major victory for the United States and its allies
C.  Led to the escalation of U.S. military involvement in Vietnam

D.     Prompted the United States to withdraw its forces from Vietnam

Answer: A

49. The purpose of the Homestead Act of 1862 was what?

   A.    To encourage western migration by providing settlers with 160 acres of public land
   B.    To provide financial aid to farmers during the Great Depression
   C.    To establish Native American reservations in the West
   D.    To outlaw slavery in new western territories

Answer: A

50. The Tea Party movement that emerged in 2009 was primarily concerned with:

   A.    Promoting civil rights and racial equality
   B.    Reducing government spending and taxes
   C.    Expanding healthcare coverage and access
   D.    Advocating for immigration reform

Answer: B

51. Which of the following best describes the United States foreign policy during the 1920s?

   A.    Interventionism
   B.    Isolationism
   C.    Containment
   D.    Appeasement

Answer: B

52. The Scopes Trial of 1925 highlighted the tensions between:

    A.    Science and religion
    B.    Labor and capital
    C.    Urban and rural populations
    D.    Prohibitionists and anti-Prohibitionists

Answer: A

53. The term "baby boom" refers to:

    A.    The significant increase in birth rates following World War II
    B.    The widespread use of birth control during the 1960s
    C.    The rapid population growth in developing countries during the 20th century
    D.    The increase in the number of immigrants entering the United States in the late 20th century

Answer: A

54. The Cuban Missile Crisis resulted in what?

    A.    The U.S. placed an embargo on Cuba
    B.    The U.S. invaded Cuba and overthrew Castro
    C.    The U.S. and USSR came to a mutual agreement to remove nuclear weapons from Cuba
    D.    The U.S. launched a pre-emptive nuclear strike against the USSR

Answer: C

55. The term "stagflation" refers to a period characterized by:

    A.    High unemployment and high inflation
    B.    High unemployment and low inflation
    C.    Low unemployment and high inflation

D.    Low unemployment and low inflation


Answer: A

# MASTERING THE SAQ (SHORT ANSWER QUESTION)

In order to excel in the Short Answer Questions (SAQ) section of the AP US History Exam, students should concentrate on the following strategies that require them to demonstrate their understanding of historical events and effectively analyze and synthesize information.

## 1. Answering the Prompt
**To effectively answer the prompt in the Short Answer Questions (SAQ) section of the AP US History Exam, it is essential to follow these steps:**

### Step 1. Read The Prompt Carefully and Thoroughly

It is advisable to invest ample time in reading the question repeatedly, ensuring a thorough comprehension of what is being asked. Dedicate sufficient attention to this step, as there is a possibility of overlooking crucial details or subtle nuances that can impact your response. If necessary, underline or highlight key phrases or words to help you focus on the critical elements of the prompt.

For example, *"Explain how the Progressive Era reforms impacted the federal government's role in the United States."*

In this given example, it is recommended to underline or highlight significant phrases such as **"Progressive Era," "reforms," "role of the federal government,"** and **"United States."** By emphasizing these key terms, you can ensure a clear focus on the specific aspects that need to be addressed in your response.

### Step 2. Identify Keywords and Essential Tasks

Once you thoroughly understand the prompt, identify the keywords and tasks that must be addressed in your response. Keywords often include historical terms, periods, events, or concepts. Essential tasks refer to the specific actions the prompt requires you to take in your answer, such as explaining, comparing, or evaluating.

**Using the same example:**

**Keywords:** Progressive Era, reforms, the federal government, United States

**Essential Tasks:** Explain the impact of Progressive Era reforms on the federal government's role

## Step 3. Ensure Your Response Directly Addresses the Question

As you begin to write your response, make sure that it directly addresses the question and stays focused on the topic. Avoid adding unrelated information or digressing into unrelated topics, as this will not help you earn points and may detract from your overall score.

For instance, in the example prompt above, your response should focus on explaining the impact of Progressive Era reforms on the federal government's role in the United States. Avoid discussing other time periods or unrelated reforms.

## Step 4. Avoid Straying from the Topic

It is crucial to stay on topic throughout your response. Going off on tangents or providing irrelevant information can strengthen your answer and make it easier for the grader to follow your argument. Revisit the prompt as you write to ensure you address the question and stay focused on the main topic.

By following these steps when answering the prompt, you will be able to create a clear, focused, and relevant response that demonstrates your understanding of the historical topic and directly addresses the question being asked.

## 2. Provide Evidence
Providing evidence is crucial to support your arguments and demonstrate your understanding of the historical topic in the Short Answer Questions (SAQ) section of the AP US History Exam.

**Here are some guidelines to effectively provide evidence in your response:**

### • Use Specific Examples from the Course Material

Draw from the information you learned during the course to provide specific examples that support your argument. In evaluating the influence of Progressive Era reforms on the federal government's role, it becomes crucial to integrate relevant examples that are specific to the topic. Considerations of notable advancements, such as the establishment of the Federal Reserve System, the introduction of income tax through the 16th Amendment, and the formation of regulatory agencies like the Food and Drug Administration, can be analyzed to illustrate the impact. These illustrations effectively exhibit the concrete influence of Progressive Era reforms on molding the functions and responsibilities of the federal government in the United States.

### • Incorporate Relevant Historical Facts and Figures

Include relevant historical facts and figures to strengthen your response. This shows that you have a solid understanding of the material and can use specific details to support your argument.

Continuing with the Progressive Era example, you could mention specific years for establishing the Federal Reserve System (1913) or ratifying the 16th Amendment (1913).

### • Connect Examples to the Broader Historical Context

Show how your examples connect to broader historical trends, themes, or events. This demonstrates your ability to synthesize information and think critically about the material.

For instance, you could explain how the Progressive Era reforms reflected a shift in public opinion towards a more active federal government, which was a response to the problems created by rapid industrialization and urbanization.

### • Ensure That Evidence Supports Your Answer

Ensure that the evidence you provide directly supports your answer and is relevant to the question. The evidence should strengthen your argument and make your response more convincing.

For example, when discussing the impact of Progressive Era reforms on the federal government's role, ensure that each example you provide (such as the Federal Reserve System or the 16th Amendment) clearly illustrates how these reforms expanded or changed the role of the federal government.

If followed carefully and consistently, these guidelines will help you provide strong and relevant evidence in your response. Remember that evidence provides the foundation for any effective argument, so make sure that it plays a central role in your answer.

## 3. Structure Your Response
**To foster the creation of a response that is well-structured and organized, it is advisable to follow these sequential steps:**

### Step 1. Organize Your Thoughts Before Writing

Before you start writing, take a few moments to organize your thoughts and create a basic outline. This will help you ensure that your response is coherent and that your ideas flow another. An outline can also help you identify gaps in your argument or areas needing more evidence.

### Step 2. Use a Clear and Concise Writing Style

Write your response using clear and concise language. Avoid using complex or overly academic language, as it can make your argument harder to follow. Strive for writing that is clear and straightforward. This will help the grader better comprehend your ideas.

### Step 3. Present Information in a Logical Order

Arrange your answer in a coherent and rational sequence to ensure a seamless transition from one argument to the next. This makes it easier for the grader to follow your argument and understand how your points connect. A logical order also helps demonstrate your ability to think critically and present a coherent argument.

### Step 4. Follow a Recommended Format

Follow the recommended format for structuring your response, such as the ACE method (Answer, Cite, Explain). This method involves providing a direct answer to the prompt, citing specific evidence to support your answer, and then explaining how that evidence supports your point. Following a consistent format makes it easier for the grader to understand your argument and assess your response.

### A well-structured response using the ACE method would look something like this:

### Answer (A):

*The First Great Awakening contributed to the development of a distinct American identity during the colonial period by promoting religious diversity, fostering democratic ideals, and creating a shared religious experience among the colonists.*

### Cite (C):

- **Religious Diversity:** The Great Awakening directly resulted in the emergence of multiple religious denominations, such as Baptists, Methodists, and Presbyterians, and consequently witnessed a significant expansion in their respective followers. These newly established religious factions played a pivotal role in contesting the dominant authority held by the Anglican Church and the Congregational Church within the colonies.
- **Democratic Ideals:** The Great Awakening emphasized personal religious experience and the notion that individuals could have a direct relationship with God. This challenged traditional religious authority and encouraged the questioning of established institutions, fostering democratic ideals.
- **Shared Religious Experience:** The revivals and emotional preaching during the Great Awakening were experienced by many colonists across different regions, creating a shared religious experience that transcended regional differences.

## Explain (E):

- The religious diversity resulting from the First Great Awakening allowed for greater religious freedom and tolerance, which differentiated American society from the more religiously homogenous European countries. The newfound religious freedom became an integral component of the emerging American identity.
- The democratic ideals fostered by the First Great Awakening contributed to developing an American identity rooted in individualism and questioning established authority. These ideals would later play a significant role in shaping the political foundations of the United States.
- The shared religious experience created during the First Great Awakening helped bridge the colonies' cultural and regional differences. This collective experience allowed the colonists to view themselves as distinct and united people, further solidifying the development of a uniquely American identity during the colonial period.

## Step 5. Stay Within the Word Limit or the Suggested Number of Sentences

Finally, adhere to the word limit or the suggested number of sentences provided in the exam instructions. Failure to adhere to these limitations may lead to penalties or complicate the grader's task of evaluating your response. By staying within the prescribed guidelines, you showcase your proficiency in effectively and succinctly conveying your ideas.

## The final answer should look like this:

*"In the colonial era, the First Great Awakening exerted a substantial influence in shaping a distinctive American identity. Achieving this transformation was made possible through the instrumental promotion of religious diversity, cultivation of democratic ideals, and establishment of a communal religious experience among the colonists. The Great Awakening directly resulted in the emergence of multiple religious denominations, such as Baptists, Methodists, and Presbyterians, and consequently witnessed a significant expansion in their respective followers. These newly established religious factions played a pivotal role in contesting the dominant authority held by the Anglican Church and the Congregational Church within the colonies. The newfound religious freedom became an integral component of the*

*emerging American identity. Additionally, the Great Awakening emphasized personal religious experience and the notion that individuals could have a direct relationship with God. This challenged traditional religious authority and encouraged the questioning of established institutions, fostering democratic ideals that would later play a significant role in shaping the political foundations of the United States. Lastly, the revivals and emotional preaching during the Great Awakening were experienced by many colonists across different regions, creating a shared religious experience that transcended regional differences and allowed the colonists to view themselves as a distinct and united people, further solidifying the development of a uniquely American identity during the colonial period."*

The answer starts by outlining three primary manners in which the First Great Awakening impacted the establishment of the American identity: by encouraging religious plurality, cultivating democratic principles, and fostering a collective religious experience. It then provides specific examples and evidence for each point, such as the establishment of various denominations, the emphasis on personal religious experience, and the widespread revivals and emotional preaching. By directly addressing the question, citing relevant examples and evidence, and clearly explaining the connections between the First Great Awakening and the development of American identity, the response demonstrates a strong understanding of the historical topic and effectively answers the prompt.

Structuring your response can also make staying within the word limit easier. Apart from employing the ACE method, it is crucial to consider paragraph length and adhere to capitalization rules. Additionally, it is recommended to avoid the usage of symbols, abbreviations, and foreign words. Graders assume that you have conducted thorough research, and they would rather deduct points for improper formatting than deny you the opportunity to answer the question.

## SAMPLE QUESTIONS AND MODEL ANSWERS
**Question:** *"Assess the Constitutional ratification's impact, delve into the Federalist Papers' influence within the United States."*

**Answer:**

*"Comprising 85 essays, the influential Papers—authored by Alexander Hamilton, James Madison, and John Jay, writing collectively as Publius—left a lasting imprint on the ratification of the United States Constitution, exerting substantial sway. These essays had a significant influence on the ratification procedure. The Federalist Papers were a full defense of the proposed Constitution. The response delved into the government's structure and advocated for the advantages of a robust central authority. The comprehensive analysis found in The Federalist Papers skillfully addressed the concerns of the anti-Federalists, highlighting the multiple advantages of the Constitution. Through critical examination, The Federalist Papers dissected the perils of despotism, concurrently providing a lucid elucidation of the mechanisms of checks and balances and the separation of powers. These mechanisms aimed to forestall any branch of government from accruing undue authority. Additionally, the Papers accentuated the indispensable function of a strong central government in preserving national security, fostering economic well-being, and upholding stability. By actively addressing raised concerns and assuming a central role in influencing public sentiment, The Federalist Papers effectively ensured the ratification of the United States Constitution."*

The response effectively presents a concise overview of the significance of the Federalist Papers in shaping the ratification of the United States Constitution. It highlights three key elements of their influence: a robust defense of the proposed document, addressing structural concerns, and advocating for a strong central government. Furthermore, it acknowledges the papers' profound impact on the ratification process.

**Question:** *"Investigate the ramifications and consequences of the Monroe Doctrine to discern its significance and the ensuing impact it had on American foreign policy during the 1800s."*

**Answer:**

*"During the 19th century, the influential Monroe Doctrine, proclaimed by James Monroe in 1823, left an enduring and substantial imprint on American foreign policy. By firmly solidifying the United States' dominion in the Western Hemisphere, this doctrine assumed a pivotal position in discouraging unwanted European interference while concurrently nurturing a profound sentiment of nationalistic pride. By explicitly stating that any aggression towards newly independent nations in the Americas*

*would be considered European interference or colonization, the Monroe Doctrine firmly established America's regional dominance. It emphasized the nation's unique responsibility to promote and safeguard democracy in the Americas, thereby influencing its approach to the Western Hemisphere, relationships with European countries, and even national identity. Moreover, the Monroe Doctrine instilled pride among Americans, both in their country's global role and domestic aspirations. In essence, the lasting impact of the Monroe Doctrine on American foreign policy highlights its pivotal role and influence in international affairs."*

The response aptly addresses the prompt by providing a focused discussion on the impact of the Monroe Doctrine on American foreign policy in the 19th century. Three main ways are identified in which the doctrine influenced foreign policy: asserting influence sphere of the United States, intervention discouraging Europeans, and promoting nationalism American. These points are then supported by specific examples and evidence, including the announcement by President James Monroe of the doctrine in 1823 and its role in asserting the unique nation's role in promoting and protecting democracy.

# EXCELLING IN THE DBQ (DOCUMENT-BASED QUESTION)

Excelling in the DBQ (Document-Based Question) in AP US History requires mastering a variety of skills.

Here's a breakdown of each step to guide you through the process:

## 1. Analyze the Documents
Begin by carefully reading and examining each document provided. Take notes on the main ideas, historical context, and the author's point of view. This will help you understand the document's relevance to the prompt and how they connect to your argument.

For example, if you were given a set of documents related to the American Revolution, you might note the perspective of British officials, American colonists, and neutral third parties. Understanding these different perspectives will help you form a well-rounded argument.

## 2. Craft a Thesis
Your thesis should clearly and concisely answer the prompt while also establishing the foundation for your argument. Ensure that your thesis is specific, defensible, and addresses all parts of the question. It should serve as a roadmap for your essay, guiding both your analysis of the documents and your incorporation of outside knowledge.

For example, if the prompt asks you to "**Evaluate the extent to which the American Revolution changed political, economic, and social structures in the colonies,**" your thesis might be: "**The American Revolution significantly changed political, economic, and social structures in the colonies by promoting democratic principles, fostering economic independence, and encouraging social reform.**"

### 3. Develop an Argument

Once you have a solid thesis, outline your argument by organizing the documents and outside information into categories that support your thesis. Consider using a combination of the chronological and thematic organization to present a clear and coherent argument.

For example, you could organize your argument into three sections: political changes, economic changes, and social changes. Use the documents and your outside knowledge to support your thesis within each section.

### 4. Use Evidence from the Documents

Incorporate evidence from the documents in your essay to support your argument. Be sure to quote or paraphrase directly from the documents and provide the proper citations (e.g., Document A, Document B). Elaborate on the relevance of the evidence presented and its link to your thesis. Remember to analyze the author's point of view and historical context for a more nuanced understanding of the document.

For example, when discussing political changes during the American Revolution, you might use a quote from Document A, written by a British official, to illustrate the British perspective on colonial governance. Explain how this perspective contrasts with the growing desire for self-governance among the colonists, as evidenced by Document B, written by a colonial leader.

### 5. Incorporate Outside Knowledge

In addition to using evidence from the documents, bring in relevant outside information to strengthen your argument. This can include historical events, people, or concepts not explicitly mentioned in the documents but that is relevant to your thesis. Integrating outside knowledge demonstrates a deeper understanding of the topic and can earn you higher points on the DBQ.

For example, when discussing economic changes during the American Revolution, you could mention the Navigation Acts, which restricted colonial trade, and the impact of the Revolution on trade policies and economic independence.

## 6. Write a Strong Introduction

Your introduction should set the stage for your essay by providing historical context and introducing your thesis. Start with a brief overview of the period or event, then transition to your thesis statement. This approach will engage the reader and give them a clear sense of your essay's direction.

### A great introduction for the prompt would be:

*"During the period preceding the American Revolution, the relationship between the British Empire and its colonies in America grew increasingly tense, leading to a confrontation for independence. As colonial society grappled with political, economic, and social transformation challenges, the revolution spurred significant changes in various aspects of life. The focal point of this essay is the assertion that the American Revolution significantly transformed the political, economic, and social systems of the colonies. The revolution accomplished this by advancing democratic ideals, stimulating economic self-sufficiency, and inspiring reform on social issues."*

This introduction provides historical context by mentioning the tensions between the British Empire and its American colonies, and it introduces the main argument by outlining the three areas of change that the essay will explore. The thesis statement is precise and unambiguous, thereby simplifying the reader's comprehension of the essay's orientation.

## 7. Write Well-Structured Body Paragraphs

Each body paragraph should focus on one aspect of your thesis and incorporate evidence from the documents and outside knowledge to support your argument. Begin each paragraph with a clear topic sentence that establishes the main idea, and then use evidence to support your claims. Analyze the evidence, explaining its significance and how it connects to your thesis. Lastly, ensure that each paragraph flows logically and coherently by using transitions between ideas and maintaining a consistent structure.

### For example, if you were writing a body paragraph about political changes during the American Revolution, your structure might look like this:

- **Topic Sentence:** The American Revolution led to a significant shift in political power, with the colonies embracing democratic principles and self-governance.

- **Evidence from Documents:** Quote or paraphrase from Document A (British perspective) and Document B (Colonial perspective) to illustrate differing views on governance.
- **Analysis:** Explain how the contrasting perspectives in the documents highlight the shift toward democratic values and self-governance in the colonies.
- **Outside Knowledge:** Discuss the establishment of the Continental Congress and drafting of the Declaration of Independence as examples of the colonies' move toward democratic governance.
- **Conclusion and Transition:** Summarize the main points of the paragraph and transition to the next topic, such as economic changes during the American Revolution.

By following this structure, your body paragraphs will be well-organized and focused, making your overall argument stronger and more persuasive.

By following this structure, your body paragraphs will be well-organized and focused, making your overall argument stronger and more persuasive.

## 8. Write a Compelling Conclusion

To craft a compelling conclusion to your essay, you should recap your central ideas, restate your thesis using different phrasing, and bring closure to your essay by providing a final thought or comment. This is your final opportunity to leave a lasting impression on the reader and demonstrate the significance of your argument. In addition to restating your thesis, briefly revisit the main points from your body paragraphs, and consider discussing the broader implications of your argument or its relevance to current events or future developments.

**For example, this could be the end of an essay about how the American Revolution changed politics, the economy, and society:**

*"In conclusion, the American Revolution marked a turning point in the colonies, as it brought about significant political, economic, and social transformations. By embracing democratic principles, asserting economic independence, and encouraging social reform, the colonies laid the foundation for a new nation founded on liberty and equality. These changes reshaped colonial society and continue to influence the development and evolution of the United States today. As we reflect on the legacy of*

*the American Revolution, it is essential to recognize the ongoing struggle to uphold and expand these democratic ideals in the face of modern challenges."*

This conclusion effectively restates the thesis, revisits the main points, and considers the broader implications of the argument, leaving the reader with a lasting impression of the essay's significance.

## The final essay should look like this:

Title: The Transformation of Colonial Society During the American Revolution

*"During the period preceding the American Revolution, the relationship between the British Empire and its colonies in America grew increasingly tense, leading to a confrontation for independence. As colonial society grappled with political, economic, and social transformation challenges, the revolution spurred significant changes in various aspects of life. The focal point of this essay is the assertion that the American Revolution significantly transformed the political, economic, and social systems of the colonies. The revolution accomplished this by advancing democratic ideals, stimulating economic self-sufficiency, and inspiring reform on social issues."*

*The American Revolution led to a significant shift in political power, with the colonies embracing democratic principles and self-governance. Document A, written by a British official, expresses the British perspective on colonial governance, which contrasts sharply with the growing desire for self-governance among the colonists, as evidenced by Document B, written by a colonial leader. This transformation is also illustrated through the establishment of the Continental Congress and the composition of the Declaration of Independence, which affirmed the colonies' entitlement to democratic self-rule. The revolution thus created an environment in which democratic ideals could take root and flourish in the new nation.*

*The American Revolution also fostered economic independence in the colonies as they sought to break free from British trade restrictions and establish their own economic policies. Documents C and D highlight the economic challenges faced by the colonies during the revolution, such as the impact of the Navigation Acts, which limited colonial trade with other nations. The revolution enabled the colonies to establish new trade relationships and develop domestic industries, paving the way for economic growth and self-sufficiency in the years to come.*

*Finally, the American Revolution encouraged social reform, as the ideals of liberty and equality inspired movements to challenge traditional hierarchies and promote greater inclusivity. Document E illustrates the growing awareness of social inequality in colonial society, while Document F showcases the efforts of reformers to address these issues. The revolution inspired movements to abolish slavery, expand women's rights, and improve conditions for the working class, reflecting the broader social changes that emerged during this transformative period.*

*"In conclusion, the American Revolution marked a turning point in the colonies, as it brought about significant political, economic, and social transformations. By embracing democratic principles, asserting economic independence, and encouraging social reform, the colonies laid the foundation for a new nation founded on liberty and equality. These changes reshaped colonial society and continue to influence the development and evolution of the United States today. As we reflect on the legacy of the American Revolution, it is essential to recognize the ongoing struggle to uphold and expand these democratic ideals in the face of modern challenges."*

By following the steps outlined above, this essay demonstrates a clear and well-supported argument, effectively addressing the prompt and incorporating evidence from both the provided documents and outside knowledge. The well-structured body paragraphs and compelling introduction and conclusion contribute to a cohesive and persuasive essay that showcases a deep understanding of the topic and the skills necessary for success on the DBQ in AP US History.

## SAMPLE QUESTIONS AND MODEL ESSAY
**Prompt:** Analyze the reasons for the emergence of the Populist movement in the late nineteenth century.

Title: The Emergence of the Populist Movement in Late Nineteenth-Century America

*"In the second half of the 1800s, the United States went through big changes in its economy, society, and government. These changes were caused by the growth of industry, the spread of cities, and the growth of big businesses. Amid these transformations, the Populist movement emerged as a powerful force advocating for the interests of farmers, laborers, and other marginalized groups. This essay will argue that the emergence of the Populist movement was driven by economic hardship, the influence of the Grange and Farmers' Alliance organizations, and a growing sense of political alienation among rural Americans."*

*The primary driving force behind the emergence of the Populist movement was the economic hardship faced by farmers and laborers in the late nineteenth century. Falling crop prices, high railroad shipping costs, and crippling debt left many rural Americans struggling to make ends meet. These economic challenges were exacerbated by the deflationary monetary policy of the federal government, which favored gold over silver and further tightened credit for farmers. Frustrated by their declining fortunes, many farmers began seeking political solutions to their problems, ultimately leading to the rise of the Populist movement.*

*The Grange and Farmers' Alliance organizations played a critical role in the development of the Populist movement by providing a platform for farmers to voice their concerns and advocate for change. These organizations, which initially focused on promoting social and educational activities among rural Americans, eventually turned their attention to more explicitly political issues, such as railroad regulation and currency reform. Through the unification of farmers and other rural citizens over these shared issues, the Grange and Farmers' Alliance established the foundation for the growth of the Populist movement as a significant political influence.*

*Finally, a growing sense of political alienation among rural Americans contributed to the rise of the Populist movement. As big business and urban centers gained increasing influence in national politics, many farmers and laborers felt left behind and ignored by the two major political parties, the Democrats and the Republicans. This dissatisfaction with the existing political system led many rural Americans to join the Populist movement, which promised to represent their interests and challenge the dominance of big business and urban elites in American politics.*

*"In conclusion, the emergence of the Populist movement in the late nineteenth century was driven by a combination of economic hardship, the influence of the Grange and Farmers' Alliance organizations, and a growing sense of political alienation among rural Americans. The movement's focus on the interests of farmers, laborers, and other marginalized groups resonated with many Americans who felt left behind by the rapid transformations of the era. Although the Populist movement ultimately failed to achieve many of its goals, its legacy can still be seen in the ongoing struggle for economic justice and political representation in the United States."*

The essay is structured to expose readers to a broad range of ideas and perspectives while also demonstrating an understanding of the historical events that led to the emergence of the Populist movement in the late nineteenth century. The introduction of this essay creates a framework by emphasizing how significant transformations in economics, society, and politics transpired during this era and how these developments prepared the way for a novel political movement. The body paragraphs then examine three contributing factors to the emergence of the Populist movement: economic hardship, the influence of the Grange and Farmers' Alliance organizations, and a growing sense of political alienation among rural Americans. By addressing each factor in turn, this essay makes clear connections between its points, which ultimately strengthens its overall argument that these three factors led to the emergence of the Populist movement. Finally, the conclusion highlights some of the key accomplishments and failures of the Populist movement before offering a nuanced discussion about how its legacy continues to influence American politics today.

**Prompt 2:** Assess the effectiveness of the Progressive movement in dealing with economic, political, and social challenges in the United States from the late 1800s to the early 1900s.

Title: The Impact of the Progressive Movement in Late Nineteenth and Early Twentieth-Century America

*"The United States confronted a host of social, political, and economic challenges at the turn of the 20th century, caused by the rapid industrialization, urbanization, and the expansion of large corporations. The Progressive movement emerged in response to these challenges, with reformers seeking to address the problems associated with*

the Gilded Age and improve the lives of ordinary Americans. This essay will argue that the Progressive movement was successful to a large extent in addressing social, political, and economic issues but that some areas remained unaddressed or saw limited progress.

The Progressive movement was notably successful in enacting social reforms aimed at improving public health, education, and working conditions. Progressive reformers like Jane Addams and Florence Kelley worked to establish settlement houses, like Hull House, which provided social services, education, and healthcare to impoverished urban residents. Additionally, the movement led to the passage of child labor laws, the introduction of workplace safety regulations, and the establishment of the Food and Drug Administration, which helped protect consumers from unsafe products.

Progressive reformers also sought to address political corruption and increase democratic participation in the United States. The movement led to the implementation of various political reforms, such as the direct primary, the initiative, the referendum, and the recall, which aimed to increase citizen involvement in the political process. The Progressive movement's endeavors to promote greater public engagement in democracy yielded two key achievements: the 17th Amendment, which permitted direct election of senators, and the 19th Amendment, which granted women the right to vote.

The Progressive movement achieved some success in addressing economic inequality and corporate power. Reformers like Theodore Roosevelt and Woodrow Wilson implemented policies to oversee large corporations, such as the Sherman Antitrust Act and the Clayton Antitrust Act, which aimed to disintegrate monopolies and encourage competition. The development of the Federal Reserve System and the adoption of the 16th Amendment, which permitted the federal income tax, supported the stabilization of the economy and the financing of government initiatives.

Despite its successes, the Progressive movement had limitations in fully addressing social, political, and economic issues. Some groups, like African Americans and immigrants, did not benefit as much from the movement's reforms, and racial segregation and discrimination persisted. Additionally, the movement could have *been more successful in addressing income inequality, as the gap between the rich and the poor continued to widen during this period.*

*To sum up, the Progressive movement was considerably effective in tackling the economic, political, and social problems that troubled the United States in the late 1800s and early 1900s. Through various reforms, the movement improved public health, education, working conditions, and democratic participation and made strides in regulating big business and stabilizing the economy. However, the movement's limitations, particularly in addressing racial inequalities and income disparity, highlight the continued need for further reform in the pursuit of a more equitable and just society."*

This essay emphasizes how the Populists and Progressives were both politically active, but the essay argues that it was the Progressives who were successful in enacting reforms that addressed income inequality and political corruption. The body paragraphs of this essay contrast the Populists and Progressives in terms of social, economic, and political factors that led to their emergence. The introduction briefly describes the context for the Progressive movement before it was introduced by examining the Populists' rise, but it does not go into detail about how each group impacted American politics. Instead, it notes that both groups were politically active and details their accomplishments in different areas but then goes on to establish a distinction between the two movements by highlighting how certain fields fell short of significant reform.

# TACKLING THE LEQ (LONG ESSAY QUESTION)

L EQ can be intimidating for any student. A strategic approach often proves paramount in conquering challenging endeavors. Here, I present a compendium of keystone tactics to assist you throughout your journey, from inception to culmination.

## 1. Choose the Option You're Most Comfortable With

Select the option that best aligns with your U.S. history knowledge and understanding. Consider the time periods and themes you feel most confident discussing and make a strategic decision based on your strengths.

For instance, if you have a strong grasp of early American history and are comfortable analyzing the factors surrounding the American Revolution, Option 1 might be your best choice.

## 2. Time Management

Allocate your time wisely. Keep in mind the time constraint for completing the LEQ, necessitating the allocation of ample time for various stages like brainstorming, outlining, writing, and revising your essay. An advisable strategy could involve dedicating approximately 10 minutes to brainstorming and outlining, 30-35 minutes to writing, and 5-10 minutes to reviewing and revising.

## 3. Brainstorm and Outline
### Before you begin writing:

- Take a few moments to brainstorm and organize your thoughts.
- Jot down key ideas, events, or individuals that are relevant to the question prompt.
- Create a brief outline that includes your thesis statement, main points, and supporting evidence. This will help you stay focused and maintain a logical flow in your essay.

For example, your prompt is *"Analyze the causes and consequences of the American Revolution."* Your outline might include your thesis statement: *"The American Revolution was primarily caused by a combination of economic, political, and social factors, and its consequences led to the establishment of a new nation with a democratic government and an evolving identity."*

## 4. Write a Strong Thesis Statement

A strong thesis statement is crucial for the success of your LEQ, as it sets the tone and direction for your entire essay. It serves as a roadmap for your reader, guiding them through your argument and signaling what they can expect from your analysis.

**To write a strong thesis statement, follow these guidelines:**

a. **Directly address the question prompt:** Ensure that your thesis statement directly answers the prompt and is clear and specific. It should demonstrate your understanding of the topic and the key issues you will be discussing.

b. **Take a clear stance:** A strong thesis statement presents a clear argument or position on the topic. Avoid making vague or overly general statements, and instead, make a definitive claim that you will support with evidence throughout your essay.

c. **Outline your main points:** While you don't need to go into extensive detail, your thesis statement should briefly overview the main points or sub-arguments you will use to support your overall argument. This helps your reader understand the structure of your essay and anticipate the evidence and analysis you will present.

## 5. Use Evidence and Analysis Effectively

In your essay, support your thesis statement with specific examples, evidence, and analysis. To substantiate your claims effectively, draw upon historical facts, events, and notable individuals. Ensure to elucidate the significance of each piece of evidence, emphasizing its connection to your overarching argument.

**Be sure to:**

## a. Use a Variety of Sources

Draw on different types of evidence, such as primary and secondary sources, to demonstrate your understanding of the topic and provide a well-rounded analysis. This can include documents, speeches, letters, and more contemporary historical interpretations.

## b. Avoid Excessive Summarization

While providing context is essential, analyze their significance before simply recounting historical events. Focus on explaining how the evidence supports your thesis and contributes to your overall argument.

## c. Address Counterarguments

Acknowledging counterarguments or alternate interpretations of the evidence can strengthen your argument. Briefly address these opposing viewpoints and explain why your argument is more persuasive or accurate.

## 6. Maintain a Clear Structure and Organization

Composing a well-organized essay enhances its readability and comprehensibility. Begin with an introduction that outlines your thesis statement. Next, create body paragraphs that each concentrate on a specific idea or sub-argument that bolsters your thesis. Finally, conclude your essay with a powerful conclusion that recaps your primary points and reinforces your argument.

**For example, you can write your essay like this:**

**Introduction:**

- Introduce the topic and provide any necessary background information.
- Present your thesis statement, which directly addresses the question prompt and outlines your main points.

For instance, if we consider the prompt *"Analyze the causes and consequences of the American Revolution,"* an introductory paragraph could provide contextual information about the events preceding the revolution and subsequently present a thesis statement:

*"The genesis of the American Revolution can be attributed to a confluence of economic, political, and social factors. These included grievances over taxation without representation, the profound impact of Enlightenment ideas on political thought, and a mounting sense of colonial discontentment with British dominion. The consequences of this revolution were far-reaching, culminating in the birth of a new nation characterized by a democratic government, a distinct political identity, and a society that fostered the development of progressive notions of freedom and equality."*

## Body Paragraphs:

- Organize your body paragraphs logically, with each paragraph focusing on a specific point or sub-argument in support of your thesis.
- At the start of each paragraph, draft a topic sentence that articulates the paragraph's principal objective in a transparent and straightforward manner.
- Provide specific evidence and analysis to support your claims, drawing on a variety of sources and avoiding excessive summarization.
- Address counterarguments or alternate interpretations of the evidence when appropriate, and explain why your argument is more persuasive or accurate.
- 

## For example, you can write the body paragraphs like this:

## Body Paragraph 1: (Discuss the economic factors leading to the American Revolution)

*"A pivotal economic factor that significantly contributed to the American Revolution encompassed the imposition of several taxes by the British government upon the colonies. Prominent examples included the Stamp Act, the Townshend Acts, and the Tea Act. The enforcement of these taxes without granting colonial representation in the British Parliament evoked deep-seated resentment among the colonists, subsequently precipitating widespread protests and boycotts as a form of resistance. The colonists argued that taxation without representation violated their rights as British subjects, which ultimately helped ignite the revolutionary movement."*

**Body Paragraph 2: (Discuss the political factors leading to the American Revolution)**

*"Political factors also played a crucial role in the American Revolution. The impact of the Enlightenment on political thought permeated the minds of numerous colonists, prompting them to challenge the legitimacy of monarchical governance and advocate for heightened political self-governance. Eminent figures such as John Locke and Thomas Paine played pivotal roles in this ideological transformation through their influential writings on topics like natural rights, social contracts, and the significance of popular sovereignty. These concepts found resonance with numerous colonists, who initiated a call for a more democratic form of governance and more extensive representation in decision-making procedures."*

**Body Paragraph 3: (Discuss the social factors leading to the American Revolution)**

*"Social factors, such as growing colonial resentment against British rule, also contributed to the American Revolution. A prevailing sentiment among colonists was a deep-seated perception of unfair treatment and exploitation at the hands of the British government, intensifying the already strained relations between the two parties. Moreover, the influential presence of revolutionary leaders like Samuel Adams and Patrick Henry served as catalysts, rallying and invigorating the colonists to actively confront British authority. This fervor led to seminal episodes in history, such as the Boston Tea Party and the convening of the First Continental Congress."*

**Conclusion:**

- Summarize your main points and reinforce your argument.
- Provide a sense of closure by connecting your argument to broader themes or historical trends.

**An illustrative instance would be crafting the conclusion in the following manner:**

*"In a nutshell, the birth of the American Revolution can be ascribed to the confluence of economic, political, and social elements, ultimately leading to its genesis. The imposition of burdensome taxes, the permeation of Enlightenment political ideas, and the mounting discontent among colonists towards British authority all played*

*significant roles in fueling the revolutionary fervor. Consequently, a novel nation with a distinct political identity and a government rooted in democracy materialized as a product of the revolution. The enduring ramifications of this upheaval are still observable in the contemporary United States, where the nation persistently grapples with evolving concepts of liberty, equality, and the government's societal role."*

## 7. Review and Revise Your Essay

Once you have finished your initial draft, it is crucial to allocate time for reviewing and revising your essay. This step is paramount in guaranteeing that your essay is well-crafted, coherent, and refined.

## To facilitate this process, consider following these guidelines:

### a. Check for Clarity and Organization

- Reread your essay, ensuring that your ideas are clearly presented, and your argument flows logically from one point to the next.
- Ensure that your thesis statement is clearly stated and effectively supported throughout the essay.
- Verify that each body paragraph begins with a topic sentence and includes appropriate evidence and analysis to support your claims.

### b. Improve Sentence Structure and Word Choice

- Look for ways to vary your sentence structure and avoid repetition.
- Choose precise, specific words to convey your ideas, and avoid using vague or overly complex language.
- Remove any unnecessary words or phrases that do not contribute to your argument or improve clarity.
- Carefully proofread your essay to identify and correct any grammar, spelling, or punctuation errors.

### c. Strengthen Your Argument and Analysis

- As you review your essay, look for opportunities to strengthen your argument by adding additional evidence, refining your analysis, or addressing potential counterarguments more effectively.

- Make sure your conclusion effectively summarizes your main points and reinforces your overall argument.

By following these key tactics, you can successfully navigate the LEQ and demonstrate a thorough understanding of U.S. history, ultimately increasing your chances of earning a high score on the exam. Remember to practice your skills, stay focused, and always strive to improve your knowledge and writing abilities in order to excel in AP US History.

## SAMPLE LEQs AND MODEL ESSAYS

**Prompt 1:** *"To what extent did the Progressive Era (1890-1920) constitute a critical juncture in the history of women in the United States?"*

## Model Essay:

*"During the Progressive Era, spanning from 1890 to 1920, women in the United States underwent a pivotal chapter in their history. This epoch witnessed remarkable strides for women, encompassing the introduction of suffrage, expanded employment prospects, and pivotal social and political reform movements propelled by women.*

*During the Progressive Era, emerged a crucial moment in the fight for suffrage, the women's. Susan B. Anthony, Elizabeth Cady Stanton, and Alice Paul, pioneers exceptional, played a part vital in the suffrage movement kick-starting. This movement led eventually to the ratification of the Amendment 19th in 1920, which women the right to vote granted. This victory remarkable not only enabled political participation women's but also triggered a transformation societal notable, reshaping perceptions about engagement women's in politics.*

*Moreover, the Progressive Era witnessed a noteworthy surge in women entering the labor force, and their contributions left a significant impact. The advent of industrialization and urbanization presented abundant work opportunities for women in factories, offices, and urban settings. Influential women such as Jane Addams and Lillian Wald played instrumental roles in establishing settlement houses and other social services, extending assistance to the underprivileged urban populace and forging novel professional avenues for women in social work and public health.*

*In tandem with suffrage and employment, the Progressive Era saw the ascendancy of diverse social and political reform movements led by women. The call for temperance, championed by noteworthy figures like Carrie Nation and Frances Willard, effectively mobilized efforts to prohibit alcohol, resulting in the ratification of the 18th Amendment in 1919. The Progressive Era encapsulated a transformative period for women in the United States, marked by the emergence of influential leaders such as Ida B. Wells and Mary Church Terrell, who played pivotal roles in advocating for civil rights and social justice. These remarkable women utilized their platforms to address pressing issues such as lynching, segregation, and discrimination.*

*In conclusion, the Progressive Era represented a significant period for women, characterized by significant advancements such as the attainment of women's suffrage and increased job opportunities. Empowering women, these changes ushered in an era of increased gender equality. Achievements of these lasting and profound effects resonated in women's lives, catalysts as acting for progress further in their rights and opportunities. Additionally, they assumed a role crucial in the development of gender roles and expectations societal, both century 20th the in and future the, leaving a mark indelible on the path toward equality gender."*

## Explanation:

American history, particularly regard to the transformations profound it brought lives women's, this essay offers exploration comprehensive a of importance remarkable its Era, Progressive the of examination perceptive a with. Through analysis meticulous a of question provided the, essay the explores adeptly developments pivotal three transpired that era: the suffrage women's of progress, the movements reform political and social women-led influential of rise the, and the workforce the in women of involvement growing. By delving into these facets, the essay effectively portrays the far-reaching and lasting impacts these changes had on the lives of women throughout the Progressive Era. This comprehensive examination offers readers a more comprehensive understanding of this era of societal transformation.

**Prompt 2:** *"Investigate the effects, both domestically and internationally, of the United States' 1917 decision to enter World War I and analyze the underlying reasons for this pivotal choice."*

**Model Essay:**

*"In 1917, driven by a convergence of factors including German aggression, the need to safeguard American economic interests, and a moral obligation to uphold democratic values, the United States entered into its participation in World War I. This choice had far-reaching consequences on both domestic and international arenas, fundamentally altering the nation's global position.*

*Instances of German aggression, particularly the renewed implementation of unrestricted submarine warfare in early 1917, prominently influenced the United States' decision to join the war. These actions directly jeopardized American maritime trade, posing a substantial menace to the nation's economic stakes. Tensions escalated further with the interception of the Zimmermann Telegram, which exposed Germany's plan to forge an alliance with Mexico against the United States. These circumstances ultimately convinced President Woodrow Wilson of the imperative to enter into war to safeguard American security.*

*Furthermore, a significant driving force behind the decision to engage in war was the imperative to protect American economic interests. The nation had become deeply intertwined with the European economy, particularly the Allied powers, through trade and financial investments. American businesses and banks had extended significant loans to the Allies, and a Central Powers victory would have jeopardized these investments. Hence, with a strategic motive to safeguard its economic interests and foster global stability, the United States forged strategic alliances with the Allies. Additionally, a deep-seated moral responsibility served as a driving force for the nation to actively advocate for democracy, self-determination, and national sovereignty. President Wilson perceived the war as a chance to establish a worldwide framework that would protect democratic values and advance a novel international order rooted in these fundamental principles.*

*The decision to engage in the war brought about significant consequences for both domestic and international affairs. Domestically, the government mobilized the economy for war, implementing new policies and regulations to support the war effort. Entities like the War Industries Board and the Food Administration were established to oversee resource production and distribution. Also, the war caused big changes in society and politics, like when the Espionage and Sedition Acts were passed. These laws limited certain civil liberties to protect national security.*

*On the stage international the, position its for moment pivotal a represented war the in participation States' United The. The conflict the into States United of entry The Allies the of favor in dynamics power of reconfiguration significant a to leading, Powers Central the of downfall the in role vital a played. Consequently, the nation emerged as a prominent global force and embraced a more proactive approach in shaping international politics. Despite Points Fourteen Wilson's and Nations of League the inability the, conflicts future prevent effectively to initiatives these of endorsement unwavering Wilson's President's showcased dedication steadfast its and States United the influence global increasing the promoting to responsibility moral a and ideals democratic uphold to duty a, interests economic of protection the, aggression German including factors multiple by motivated ultimately was I War World into entrance States' United The.*

*Both affairs international and domestic for consequences-reaching far had decision This century 20th the of remainder the throughout affairs global in engagement enduring its and power global prominent a as States United the positioned it."*

## Explanation:

The essay aptly demonstrates the author's profound comprehension of the factors that propelled the United States to enter World War I and provides a comprehensive understanding of the subsequent impact on domestic and international affairs. This insightful essay provides a deep exploration of the underlying motivations behind the United States' choice to enter World War I and comprehensively examines the ensuing ramifications on both the domestic and global fronts. The essay showcases an admirable grasp of the historical backdrop and offers a thorough analysis of how the war shaped the United States' position in the international arena and its internal policies. With its well-rounded assessment, the essay effectively illustrates an understanding of the historical context and its impact on the United States' global standing and domestic affairs during World War I.

# COMPREHENSIVE CONTENT REVIEW

## Period 1: Colonial America (1491-1754)

### • Indigenous Cultures

Different ways of life developed by complex societies like the Mississippian culture, the Anasazi, the Iroquois Confederacy, and the Algonquian-speaking tribes in North America, fitting their local environments, before the Europeans arrived to the Americas, where many diverse cultures coexisted.

### • European Colonization

Following Christopher Columbus's voyages in the late 15th century, the New World witnessed European settlers arriving. Individuals hailing from Spain, France, the Netherlands, and England journeyed to the Americas, driven by the pursuit of resources, unexplored trade pathways, and territorial expansion for their respective nations. These settlers established colonies, exploiting both the land and the indigenous populations to further their own interests. One way they did this was through forced labor systems like the encomienda.

### • Jamestown

Jamestown was the first English town to stay in North America for good. It was built in 1607 in what is now Virginia. It faced numerous difficulties, including disease, famine, and wars with the Powhatan Confederacy. John Rolfe brought tobacco farming to the colony, which helped the economy grow and kept the colony alive.

### • Plymouth Colony

The Pilgrims, who were English Separatists, started the Plymouth Colony in 1620. They were looking for religious freedom. They set up an independent community based on the Mayflower Compact, which was an agreement to work together for the good of everyone.

## • The Massachusetts Bay Colony

In 1630, the Massachusetts Bay Colony was founded by English Puritans with the ambition of creating a prominent "city on a hill" that would serve as an exemplary Christian community. This colony held steadfast religious convictions and harbored a tendency to be unwelcoming towards dissenting individuals. Furthermore, it fostered a closely intertwined connection between the church and the governing authorities.

## • Colonial Economies

In each colonial region, the economies varied significantly. The New England colonies, for instance, emphasized fishing, shipbuilding, and small-scale agriculture. In contrast, the Middle Colonies were renowned for their diverse trading ventures and agricultural pursuits. As for the Southern colonies, their economic foundation heavily relied on cash crops such as tobacco, rice, and indigo, cultivated on expansive plantations through the utilization of slave labor.

## • Slavery

In colonial life, slavery held a vital position, especially in Southern regions, where the plantation system demanded a large workforce. The transatlantic trade in slaves facilitated the movement of countless Africans to the Americas, creating a hierarchical caste system based on race and leading to widespread mistreatment of those who were enslaved, subjected to coerced labor.

## • Religion

Within the colonies, a diverse array of Protestant denominations thrived, including Puritans, Anglicans, Quakers, and Baptists. There were also smaller Catholic and Jewish communities. Religion often affected colonial life, politics, and the way people lived together.

## • The Enlightenment

The Enlightenment was an intellectual movement that focused on reason, science, and being your own person. The ideas of the Enlightenment affected the way colonial people thought about politics. This led to the ideas of democracy, the separation of powers, and natural rights.

## • The Great Awakening

During the mid-18th century, the colonies underwent a significant religious resurgence referred to as the Great Awakening. This movement was characterized by the presence of itinerant preachers such as George Whitefield and Jonathan Edwards, who ignited fervent religious enthusiasm and raised critical questions regarding the authority of established religious figures. The movement led to more religious diversity and the growth of new groups. It also helped the United States develop a unique sense of who it is.

## Period 2: The Revolutionary Era (1754-1783)

### • French and Indian War

The conflict known as the Seven Years' War took place from 1754 to 1763 and pitted Britain against France. Within this larger war, the French and Indian War unfolded. One side emerged in North America, where the French and their Native American allies clashed with the British and their colonies. This conflict, resulting in the signing of the Treaty of Paris in 1763, marked the war's conclusion and granted British dominion over French territories in North America.

### • American Revolution Causes

Various economic, political, and social factors influenced the American Revolution. British policies, including taxation without representation, triggered discontent among colonists. The emergence of American identity also fueled a desire for greater autonomy. Enlightenment ideals promoting self-government, natural rights, and equality further contributed to the revolutionary spirit. These factors collectively played significant roles in causing the American Revolution.

### • Independence Declaration

On July 4, 1776, the adoption of the Declaration of Independence marked the unified decision of the 13 American colonies to break away from British rule. Thomas Jefferson, the primary author, eloquently conveyed the colonies' grievances and concerns regarding the British monarchy. Formally declaring the intent of the colonies, the Declaration of Independence marked the birth of the United States of America as a new nation, emphasizing principles such as individual rights, self-governance, and the pursuit of happiness.

## • Revolutionary War

The fierce conflict of the American Revolutionary War unraveled between 1775 and 1783 when the American colonies clashed with the British Empire. Supported by France, Spain, and the Dutch Republic, the ultimate victory was achieved by the colonists. This pivotal outcome terminated British dominance in North America and played a vital role in the formation of the United States.

## • Treaty of Paris (1783)

The conclusion of the American Revolutionary War was marked in 1783 with the Treaty of Paris. The agreement acknowledged the United States independence and set up borders between the new country and British North America.

## • Articles of Confederation

Signed in 1781, the Articles of Confederation served as the initial constitution for the United States, establishing a decentralized governance structure where the majority of authority resided within individual states. However, it swiftly became apparent that the Articles lacked the necessary efficacy. Consequently, demands for a more potent central government emerged, ultimately prompting the creation of the U.S. Constitution.

## • Constitutional Convention

With the purpose of tackling the shortcomings of the Articles of Confederation, the Constitutional Convention of 1787 unfolded in Philadelphia. Throughout this gathering, a collaborative endeavor ensued among delegates as they worked on composing and later approving the U.S. Constitution. This significant milestone laid the foundation for the country's governance and stood as a remarkable accomplishment.

# Period 3: The New Nation (1783-1820)

## • American Founding Document

Our nation's formative script, the U.S. Constitution, was greenlit in 1788 and became operative in 1789. This historic manuscript, conceived to rectify the frailties of the Articles of Confederation, stipulated the federal government's structure, dividing it into three sections: executive, legislative, and judicial. It aimed for a power equilibrium, checks and counterbalances, and safeguarded individual rights via the Bill of Rights.

## • Fundamental Rights Charter

1. The Charter of Fundamental Rights, often known as the Bill of Rights, comprises the first ten modifications to the Constitution. Approved in 1791, these revisions safeguard crucial personal freedoms, such as the ability to express oneself, practice religion, and possess firearms, among other rights.

## • Hamilton's Financial Plan

In order to stabilize the economy after the American Revolution, Secretary of Treasury Alexander Hamilton proposed a financial plan. His proposal included the federal government assuming state debts, the establishment of a national bank, and support for industries. Despite objections, notably from Thomas Jefferson who favored agrarian society, the plan was implemented, significantly bolstering the country's economic standing and encouraging growth.

## • Era of the Federalists

The Federalist Era, spanning from 1789-1801, witnessed a heated argument between Federalists, strong central government proponents, and Democratic-Republicans, state rights advocates. Supported mainly by urban and commercial elites, the Federalists contrasted with Democratic-Republicans, who were backed by rural, agrarian communities. This period was defined by deep political chasms and the birth of the two-party system.

## • John Adams' Presidency

John Adams encountered various challenges during his presidency, serving as the second president of the United States from 1797 to 1801. Notable among these trials were events such as the XYZ Affair and the enactment of the Alien and Sedition Acts. With the objective of preserving a stance of neutrality in global matters, Adams diligently worked towards averting a possible conflict with France. In the end, he signed the Convention of 1800, which ended all disputes. During his time in office, there were also problems between Federalists and Democratic-Republicans.

## • Jeffersonian Democracy

Jefferson's presidency (1801–1809) witnessed his enthusiastic embrace of Jeffersonian Democracy, an ideology highlighting agrarianism, states' rights, and a strict constitutional interpretation. Notably, during his tenure, the United States acquired the Louisiana Territory and implemented the Embargo Act of 1807, aimed at averting war but causing economic repercussions.

## • 1812 War

As a result of trade limitations, the practice of impressment of American sailors, and British support to Native American tribes, the War of 1812 erupted. Unfolding between the United States and Great Britain, this conflict, frequently referred to as the "Second War of Independence," reached its climax with the signing of the Treaty of Ghent in 1814.

## • The Era of Good Feelings

After the War of 1812, the United States experienced a period commonly referred to as the "Era of Good Feelings," spanning from 1815 to 1824. President James Monroe's term was characterized by a temporary decrease in partisan politics and a prevailing sense of national unity and purpose. Despite this, the era also saw growing sectional tensions over slavery and economic issues.

## • The Missouri Compromise

In 1820, Congress passed the Missouri Compromise, addressing the admission of Missouri as a slave state and Maine as a free state, maintaining the balance between slave states and free states. The compromise also prohibited slavery north of the 36°30′ latitude line within the Louisiana Territory.

## Period 4: The Age of Expansion and Reform (1820-1860)

### • Manifest Destiny

Manifest Destiny was a widely held belief in the 19th century that American settlers were destined to expand across the continent. This belief was used to justify the annexation of Texas, the Oregon Territory, and other western lands. It also led to conflict with Mexico and with Native American nations.

### • The Enforced Migration of Native Americans and Trail of Tears

President Andrew Jackson implemented the Indian Removal Act in 1830, which initiated the coercive relocation of numerous Indigenous nations from their longstanding territories in the Southeastern United States to designated lands west of the Mississippi River, commonly referred to as "Indian Territory." This challenging and tragic journey is recognized as the Trail of Tears.

### • Jacksonian Democracy

During President Andrew Jackson's tenure from 1829 to 1837, the era of Jacksonian Democracy highlighted the importance of the common man, a robust executive branch, and the pursuit of equality among white men. Nonetheless, this period witnessed spirited debates surrounding states' rights and the federal government's role, igniting passionate conversations and discord.

### • The Second Awakening

In the early 19th century, a notable religious resurgence known as the Second Great Awakening spread throughout the country, sparking heightened religious enthusiasm and a desire for moral reform. This significant religious revival had a profound impact on influencing a range of societal shifts, including the promotion of temperance, the movement to abolish slavery, and the advancement of women's rights.

## • The Revolutionary Shift to Market Economy

In the early 19th century, a notable economic shift called the Market Revolution unfolded in the United States, bringing about a dramatic transformation. This period witnessed a transition from an agricultural-centered economy to one propelled by industrialization and bolstered infrastructure, including canals, roads, and eventually railways. Consequently, American society underwent profound changes, with urbanization on the rise and the middle class expanding significantly.

## • Reform Movements

In American society, the synergistic impact of the Market Revolution and the Second Great Awakening ignited a surge of reform movements. These encompassed abolitionism, the women's suffrage movement, and educational reform, among various others. Visionary individuals such as Frederick Douglass, Susan B. Anthony, and Horace Mann assumed pivotal leadership roles, championing and advocating for these causes.

## • Slavery in the Antebellum South

Amidst this era, the institution of slavery became deeply entrenched within the Southern states, primarily driven by the exponential growth of cotton production facilitated by the invention of the cotton gin. Debates about the ethics of slavery and its spread into new territories amplified sectional tensions.

## • The War Between Mexico and America

The conflict known as the Mexican-American War, which took place from 1846 to 1848, emerged as a result of territorial disagreements following the annexation of Texas. This armed confrontation came to a close with the signing of the Treaty of Guadalupe Hidalgo, resulting in a significant expansion of U.S. territory that included present-day areas such as California, Nevada, Utah, Arizona, and New Mexico.

## • Compromise of 1850 and Fugitive Slave Act

The Compromise of 1850 was implemented in an effort to alleviate escalating sectional tensions. It involved the admission of California as a free state and the adoption of popular sovereignty, whereby newly acquired territories could determine the issue of slavery themselves. However, the compromise also included the controversial Fugitive Slave Act, which mandated citizens to assist in capturing runaway slaves and denied these individuals a fair trial.

## • The Kansas-Nebraska Act and the Kansas Conflict

The Kansas-Nebraska Act of 1854 permitted the territories of Kansas and Nebraska to decide on the slavery issue through popular sovereignty, effectively nullifying the Missouri Compromise line. This led to a violent conflict known as Bleeding Kansas, as forces for and against slavery clashed.

# Period 5: The Era of Civil War and Reconstruction (1860-1877)

## • Ascendancy of Abraham Lincoln

The successful election of Abraham Lincoln in 1860, driven by his opposition to slavery, evoked considerable unease among the states in the South. His ascension to the presidency served as a triggering factor for secession and signaled the beginning of the Civil War.

## • Onset of the Civil War

A pivotal chapter in the annals of American history, the Civil War, originated in 1861 and culminated in 1865. It erupted principally due to increasing discord over the authority of states and the contested issue of slavery.

## • Proclamation of Liberation

President Lincoln's Proclamation of Liberation in 1862 declared the freedom of enslaved individuals within territories held by the Confederates. While it didn't immediately liberate all enslaved individuals, it altered the essence of the war, making it a fight for human emancipation.

## • Confrontation at Gettysburg

The Confrontation at Gettysburg in 1863 emerged as a pivotal moment during the Civil War. This fiercely fought battle resulted in immense casualties for both the Union and Confederate forces. However, it ultimately concluded with a triumph for the Union, signifying a significant turning point in the war in favor of the North.

## • Murder of Abraham Lincoln

The untimely murder of Abraham Lincoln in 1865 by John Wilkes Booth, a Confederate sympathizer, occurred mere days after the Confederate surrender. His demise signified the commencement of the turbulent phase of Reconstruction.

## • Policies of Reconstruction

The era of Reconstruction, aimed at reintegrating Southern states and aiding the transition of formerly enslaved individuals to post-slavery life, was a fraught period punctuated by substantial political transformations and intense racial discord. This time saw notable achievements, such as the ratification of the 14th and 15th amendments, and setbacks, including the emergence of Black Codes and the Ku Klux Klan.

## • The Agreement of 1877

The disputed presidential election of 1876 was resolved through the Agreement of 1877, wherein Republican Rutherford B. Hayes was granted the presidency in return for the removal of federal troops from the South, effectively concluding the era of Reconstruction.

# Period 6: Industrialization and the Growth of the West (1865-1898)

## • Transcontinental Railways

The completion of the transcontinental railway system in 1869 fundamentally transformed the United States. It accelerated the settlement of the Western states, facilitated economic growth, and encouraged the movement of goods and people across the country.

## • Industrial Magnates Rise

The period witnessed the ascent of industrial moguls and influential corporations, including John D. Rockefeller's dominance in oil, Andrew Carnegie's control over the steel industry, and Cornelius Vanderbilt's influence in the railroad sector. Their innovative business methodologies revolutionized the American economic landscape, albeit creating a substantial wealth disparity.

## • Influx of Immigrants

The latter part of the 19th century was characterized by a significant surge in immigration, with numerous individuals hailing from Europe and Asia venturing to the United States in pursuit of improved prospects. These immigrants enhanced the cultural mix and labor force of the nation, despite facing hardships and prejudice.

## • Native American Opposition

During westward expansion, American settlers and armed forces faced opposition from multiple Native American tribes, including the Sioux, Apache, and Nez Perce, who vehemently resisted the encroachment upon their lands. Despite their determined resistance, the U.S. government frequently employed military action, leading to tragic incidents like the Massacre at Wounded Knee and the Battle of Little Bighorn.

## • Emergence of the Labor Movement

Industrial capitalism's rise led to the deterioration of labor conditions, prompting the establishment of labor unions and the advocacy for workers' rights. Incidents such as the Pullman Strike and the Haymarket Riot underscored the escalating friction between labor and capital.

## • Rise of the Populist Movement

Emerging towards the end of the 19th century, the Populist movement arose as a reaction to the economic hardships experienced by workers and farmers. This movement championed various reforms, such as the introduction of an income tax, the direct election of senators, and the oversight of railroad activities.

• **Urbanization and Social Changes**

Rapid industrial growth led to the rise of cities and significant social changes. Progress and poverty existed side by side, leading to philanthropy from the wealthy and social reform movements aimed at improving conditions for the urban poor.

## • Expansionism and the Spanish-American War

During the late 19th century, the United States pursued a course of imperialism motivated by strategic, economic, and ideological factors. The Spanish-American War of 1898, largely triggered by the Cuban independence movement, resulted in the acquisition of territories including the Philippines, Guam, and Puerto Rico, marking the nation's ascent as a global power.

# Period 7: The Emergence of Modern America (1890-1945)

## • Progressive Reforms

At the turn of the century, a wave of reforms collectively referred to as the Progressive Movement surfaced, with the goal of tackling social issues arising from rapid industrialization, urbanization, and immigration. Reformers focused on combating political corruption, limiting corporate control, enhancing labor rights, and promoting women's suffrage.

## • World War I

At the outbreak of World War I in 1914, the United States initially adopted a policy of neutrality. However, due to factors such as German submarine warfare and the disclosure of the Zimmerman Telegram, the U.S. was eventually compelled to enter the war in 1917 under the leadership of President Woodrow Wilson. The conflict came to an end in 1918 with the signing of the Treaty of Versailles.

## • The Roaring Twenties

The period known as the "Roaring Twenties," encompassing the 1920s, experienced significant social, cultural, and economic changes. This era was characterized by a booming economy, increased consumerism, the widespread popularity of mass culture, and notable advancements in civil rights for women and African Americans. However, it was also a time of tension between traditional values and the emergence of modernist ideologies.

## • The Great Depression

The stock market crash of 1929 acted as a trigger for the Great Depression, which stands as the most severe economic crisis in American history. Consequently, unemployment rates surged, banks failed, and a significant portion of the population was plunged into poverty. In response to these challenges, President Franklin D. Roosevelt implemented the New Deal, a set of policies designed to alleviate suffering and revive the economy.

## • New Deal Policies

President Roosevelt's New Deal comprised a diverse array of initiatives and policies intended to extend aid to those facing unemployment and poverty, stimulate economic recovery, and implement reforms within the financial sector. These endeavors involved substantial government intervention in the economy and resulted in a noteworthy shift in the dynamic between the state and its citizens.

## • World War II

World War II, a global conflict, began in 1939, and initially, the United States adopted a stance of neutrality. However, after the Japanese attack on Pearl Harbor in December 1941, the U.S. joined the war. The war effort mobilized American society, bringing an end to the Great Depression and leading to significant social transformations, including increased opportunities for women and minorities. Following the war, the United States emerged as one of the two major global powers, ushering in the Cold War era.

# Period 8: Cold War and Civil Rights Era (1945-1980)

## • The Cold War

The post-World War II era marked the emergence of two superpowers, the United States and the Soviet Union, leading to an extended period of geopolitical strain known as the Cold War. This ideological and political rivalry involved a range of activities, including arms races, proxy conflicts, and the implementation of the containment policy, which aimed to curb the expansion of communism.

## • Truman Doctrine and Marshall Plan

In 1947, the Truman Doctrine was announced, expressing the United States' dedication to providing support to nations confronting the menace of communism. Concurrently, the implementation of the Marshall Plan aimed to aid in the economic revival of Western Europe. These initiatives played a crucial role in America's strategy to contain the expansion of communism during the Cold War.

## • Korean and Vietnam Wars

The Korean War (1950-1953) and the Vietnam War (1965-1973) were notable proxy conflicts during the Cold War. These conflicts were fought to counter the expansion of communism in Asia but faced considerable domestic controversy, particularly the Vietnam War, which led to widespread protests at home.

## • Civil Rights Movement

During this period, the pursuit of racial equality gained momentum, resulting in significant social transformations. Milestones such as the Montgomery Bus Boycott, the March on Washington, and pivotal legislations like the Civil Rights Act of 1964 and the Voting Rights Act of 1965 exemplify the era's profound struggle for racial justice.

## • Feminist Movement and Other Social Changes

The post-war era witnessed a surge in social justice movements, notably the second wave of feminism that fought for women's rights, as well as the emergence of the gay rights movement. This period also marked significant cultural shifts, exemplified by the counterculture movement and the activism of youth in the 1960s and 1970s.

## • Space Race

The Space Race played a pivotal role in the Cold War, with the United States and the Soviet Union engaged in a competition for dominance in space exploration. Notable milestones included the Soviet Union's launch of Sputnik, the first artificial satellite, and the United States' achievement of landing the first human on the moon in 1969. These events underscored the technological and ideological rivalry between the two superpowers during that era.

• **Economic Changes and the Rise of Conservatism**

The post-war era witnessed remarkable economic expansion and changes in the American economy, marked by the growth of the middle class, suburbanization, and the emergence of consumer culture. However, economic difficulties in the 1970s generated discontent with liberal policies, setting the stage for the ascent of conservatism.

## Period 9: Post-Cold War and Twenty-First Century America (1980-Present)

• **The Reagan Revolution**

The election of Ronald Reagan in 1980 signified the emergence of a new conservative movement within American politics. Reagan's presidency emphasized the principles of free markets, reduced taxation, limited government regulation, and a robust national defense. During this period, the Cold War escalated under Reagan's firm anti-communist stance.

• **The End of the Cold War**

The late 1980s and early 1990s were characterized by the conclusion of the Cold War, which was punctuated by significant events like the fall of the Berlin Wall in 1989 and the subsequent dissolution of the Soviet Union in 1991. These transformative occurrences resulted in the United States emerging as the sole global superpower.

• **Globalization and the Technological Revolution**

The late 20th and early 21st centuries have been defined by a notable surge in globalization and rapid advancements in technology. The advent of the internet and other digital technologies has brought about fundamental transformations in the economy, society, and culture. These developments have interconnected people across the globe, revolutionized communication, and reshaped various aspects of human life.

• **The 9/11 Attacks and the War on Terror**

The terrorist attacks on the World Trade Center and the Pentagon on September 11, 2001, had a profound impact on both the foreign and domestic policies of the United States. These attacks prompted the initiation of the War on Terror, which involved military interventions in Afghanistan and Iraq.

### • Economic Crises

The early 21st century was marked by notable economic challenges, including the dot-com crash in 2000 and the subsequent Great Recession triggered by the 2008 financial crisis. These events resulted in widespread economic hardship and sparked extensive discussions regarding economic policies.

### • Social Changes and Movements

In the early 21st century, ongoing social and cultural changes have been observed, encompassing discussions and debates surrounding topics such as immigration, LGBT+ rights, and racial equality. This period has also witnessed the emergence of influential social movements like Black Lives Matter and MeToo, which have garnered significant attention and contributed to shaping the discourse on these issues.

### • Climate Change and Environmental Concerns

In the 21st century, the escalating concern regarding climate change and other environmental challenges has gained substantial prominence. This has sparked debates regarding environmental policies and the need to prioritize renewable energy sources. The recognition of these issues has prompted a global focus on sustainability and the exploration of strategies to mitigate the impacts of climate change and preserve the planet for future generations.

# EFFECTIVE STUDY TECHNIQUES AND TOOLS

Adopting effective study techniques and tools is crucial to excelling in the AP US History Exam. The following strategies can greatly help you in your preparation:

## 1. Utilize Flashcards, Mnemonics, and Other Memory Aids

Flashcards, mnemonics, and other memory aids are essential tools for retaining and recalling important information. They can be particularly helpful for memorizing key terms, concepts, and historical events in AP World History.

### • Flashcards

Create physical or digital flashcards with key terms, dates, and concepts on one side and their definitions or explanations on the other. You can use pre-made flashcards available online or make your own. Review your flashcards regularly to reinforce your memory and understanding of the material.

For example:

**Front:** Missouri Compromise (1820)

**Back:** *In the United States, the Missouri Compromise emerged as a federal law to address the contentious issue of slavery in the western territories. This measure provided a temporary solution by declaring Missouri a slave state and Maine a free state, ensuring a Senate power equilibrium. It also prohibited slavery north of the 36°30' parallel, except for Missouri.*

### • Mnemonics

Mnemonics are aids to memory that assist in retaining intricate information by creating uncomplicated associations or patterns. They can be particularly helpful for remembering important dates, events, or sequences. One such instance is the utilization of the acronym "HOMES" to recall the names of the Great Lakes (Huron, Ontario, Michigan, Erie, Superior).

## • Other Memory Aids

Utilizing visual aids like mind maps, diagrams, or charts can be beneficial for students in organizing and retaining information. Additionally, creating songs, poems, or stories can serve as effective mnemonic devices to aid in remembering key events or concepts.

## 2. Creating a Study Plan and Schedule

Creating a study plan and schedule for AP US History will help you manage your time effectively, cover all the necessary material, and prepare for the exam in a systematic manner.

## Here are some steps to create a successful study plan:

### Step 1: Assess Your Current Knowledge

Take a diagnostic or practice exam to identify your strengths and weaknesses. This approach will provide you with a perception of the subjects you need to prioritize and assist you in setting practical objectives.

You can do this by using online resources like Khan Academy, College Board's AP Classroom, or various AP US History textbooks that include practice exams.

### Step 2: Set Your Goals

Determine your target score for the AP US History exam. Consider your individual strengths and weaknesses, alongside the remaining time until the exam, to develop a plan that caters to your needs.

Maintain motivation and track your progress by setting both short-term and long-term goals. Suppose your objective is to attain a score of 5 on the exam. In that case, establish weekly short-term goals, such as mastering specific topics or skills, to steadily work towards your desired outcome. This targeted approach facilitates focused and gradual progress, enabling you to steadily move closer to your ultimate objective.

## Step 3: Create a Study Schedule

Divide the course content into manageable sections and allocate time to each topic based on your strengths and weaknesses. Make sure to allocate time for reviewing and practicing skills as well.

Design an effective study schedule, it's crucial to incorporate a mix of daily, weekly, and monthly objectives. Ensure that your schedule strikes a balance between being practical and adaptable, considering your academic responsibilities, extracurricular engagements, and social interactions. Don't forget to include periodic breaks and designated days off to mitigate the risk of exhaustion.

### Sample Weekly Schedule:

### Monday

- 1 hour: Review lecture notes or textbook on Colonial America
- 30 minutes: Practice multiple-choice questions on Colonial America
- 15 minutes: Review vocabulary and key terms

### Tuesday

- 1 hour: Review lecture notes or textbook on the American Revolution
- 30 minutes: Practice short-answer questions on the American Revolution
- 15 minutes: Review vocabulary and key terms

### Wednesday

- 1 hour: Review lecture notes or textbook on the Early Republic
- 30 minutes: Practice multiple-choice questions on the Early Republic
- 15 minutes: Review vocabulary and key terms

### Thursday

- 1 hour: Review lecture notes or textbook on the Age of Jackson
- 30 minutes: Practice short-answer questions on the Age of Jackson

- 15 minutes: Review vocabulary and key terms

## Friday

- 1 hour: Review lecture notes or textbook on the Civil War and Reconstruction
- 30 minutes: Practice essay questions on the Civil War and Reconstruction
- 15 minutes: Review vocabulary and key terms

Saturday

- 2 hours: Take a practice exam or focus on specific areas where you need improvement
- 1 hour: Review practice exam results and address weak areas

## Sunday

- Day off or catch-up day if needed

## Step 4: Review and Revise

Periodically review your progress and adjust your study plan as needed. Keep track of your improvements and areas that still need work. As the exam date approaches, spend more time on review and practicing and less time learning new material.

Doing these steps will prepare you for the AP US History exam. Remember to be consistent with your study schedule, make adjustments when necessary, and maintain a positive attitude throughout the process.

## 3. Prepare Mentally and Physically for the Exam

Preparing mentally and physically for the AP US History exam is just as important as mastering the content.

**To ensure you're in the best possible condition for the test, consider the following tips:**

## Mental Preparation
### a. Cultivate a Growth Mindset

Embracing the concept that your skills and intellect can improve through perseverance and diligence can foster a mindset of positivity towards challenges and interpret setbacks as opportunities for growth and development.

### b. Set Realistic Expectations

Understand that facing difficulties while studying for a challenging exam like AP US History is normal. Rather than aiming for flawlessness, center your efforts on advancing and enhancing your comprehension of the material incrementally.

### c. Practice Relaxation Techniques

Acquire the skill of managing stress and anxiety through relaxation practices such as deep breathing, meditation, and progressive muscle relaxation. These methods can help you stay calm and focused during your study sessions and on exam day.

## Breathing Techniques
### i. 4-7-8 Breathing Technique:

1. Inhale through the nose for four counts.
2. Hold your breath until the count of seven.
3. Exhale through the mouth for eight counts.
4. Repeat this cycle 4 times.

### ii. Box Breathing Technique:

1. Inhale through the nose for four counts.
2. Retain the breath for a four-second pause.
3. Exhale through the mouth for four counts.
4. Suspend your breath for a four-second interval.

5.    Iterate this sequence for a few minutes or until a sense of tranquility settles in.

## Physical Preparation:
### a. Get Regular Exercise

To infuse your routine with a harmonized blend of physical activity, intertwine it with your daily life to invigorate spirits, alleviate stress, and enhance vitality. Strive for a minimum of 150 minutes per week engaging in moderate-intensity aerobic exercises or 75 minutes of vigorous-intensity aerobic exercises. Furthermore, make it a priority to include muscle-strengthening exercises twice weekly. By integrating these practices seamlessly into your lifestyle, you can relish the benefits of an active and wholesome way of existence.

### b. Maintain a Balanced Diet

Fuel your body with a nourishing diet that encompasses a diverse range of fruits, vegetables, whole grains, lean proteins, and healthy fats. This approach will provide you with the essential energy and a sharpened mental state necessary for productive studying.

### c. Prioritize Sleep

Prioritize acquiring a restorative 7-9 hours of uninterrupted sleep every night to facilitate memory consolidation, enhance cognitive abilities, and promote overall well-being. Establish a steady sleep routine and nurture a calming bedtime ritual to optimize the quality of your sleep.

### d. Stay Hydrated

Stay hydrated and uphold prime cognitive function by consuming an adequate amount of water throughout the day. Avoid excessive caffeine and sugary drinks, as they can lead to dehydration and energy crashes.

By integrating these study strategies, utilizing helpful resources, and prioritizing self-care, you'll fortify your AP US History exam readiness and position yourself for optimal performance on test day. Maintain consistency, unwavering focus, and a positive mindset, and you'll pave the way towards attaining your desired score.

# CONCLUSION

As you approach the AP U.S. History Exam, it is essential to understand that success is rooted in consistent, focused, and effective preparation. The APUSH exam is a comprehensive test that not only assesses your knowledge of U.S. history but also challenges your ability to apply historical thinking skills and analyze a wide range of primary and secondary sources. By adequately preparing for the exam, you enhance your likelihood of achieving a superior score and cultivate a more profound appreciation and comprehension of the intricate history of the United States.

Throughout your preparation journey, remember that consistency is key. A well-structured study plan tailored to your individual strengths and weaknesses will ensure that you cover all the necessary content and practice the skills needed to excel in the exam. Utilize diverse resources, such as textbooks, review books, online materials, and practice exams, to ensure a comprehensive understanding of the subject matter. Additionally, seeking guidance and support from teachers, tutors, or classmates can provide valuable insights and help you address areas of difficulty.

Remember that practice makes perfect as you hone your skills in tackling each question type—multiple-choice, short answer, document-based, and long essay questions. The more you familiarize yourself with the format, requirements, and expectations of each question type, the more confident and capable you will become in approaching them on exam day. Focus on improving your ability to read and analyze primary and secondary sources, craft clear and concise thesis statements, develop well-structured arguments, and support your claims with relevant evidence from the documents and your own knowledge.

When preparing for exam day, it is crucial to maintain a balanced lifestyle and prioritize stress management. A combination of regular exercise, a healthy diet, and sufficient sleep can help you stay focused, energized, and ready to tackle the challenges of the APUSH exam. Furthermore, integrating relaxation techniques such as deep breathing, meditation, or progressive muscle relaxation can aid in maintaining a composed and collected demeanor in the presence of exam-related stress.

On the exam day itself, be sure to arrive well-prepared and confident in your abilities. Familiarize yourself with the exam logistics, such as the location, time, seating arrangements, and necessary materials. This will help you avoid unnecessary stress and ensure a smooth exam experience. Keep in mind that all of your hard work and dedication in getting ready has given you the knowledge and skills you need to do well.

In the end, the AP U.S. History Exam is a difficult but rewarding way to show how well you know the rich and complicated history of the United States. By focusing on consistent preparation, effective study strategies, and stress management, you can maximize your chances of earning a high score on the exam and reap the benefits of your hard work, such as earning college credits and enhancing your academic profile. As you approach the exam day, remember that your success is a testament to your dedication, perseverance, and passion for learning about the past and applying its lessons to the present and future.

# RESOURCES AND TOOLS

• *"American Pageant" by David M. Kennedy et al.*
*(https://www.amazon.com/American-Pageant-History-Advanced-Placement/dp/1305075900)*

• *"Give Me Liberty!: An American History" by Eric Foner*
*(https://www.amazon.com/Give-Me-Liberty-American-History/dp/0393615650)*

• *"Cracking the AP U.S. History Exam" by The Princeton Review*
*(https://www.amazon.com/Cracking-U-S-History-Exam-2020/dp/0525568395)*

• *Strive for a 5 for America's History: Preparing for the Ap\* U. S. History Exam by James A. Henretta, Eric Hinderaker, Rebecca Edwards, Robert Self*
*(https://www.amazon.com/Strive-Americas-History-Preparing-Exam/dp/1319065937)*

• *Khan Academy: AP U.S. History (https://www.khanacademy.org/humanities/us-history)*

• *AP Classroom: AP U.S. History (https://apcentral.collegeboard.org/courses/ap-united-states-history/classroom-resources)*

• *Quizlet - AP U.S. History (https://quizlet.com/subject/apush/)*

• *Crash Course U.S. History on YouTube*
*(https://www.youtube.com/playlist?list=PL8dPuuaLjXtMwmepBjTSG593eG7ObzO7s)*

• *Jocz Productions APUSH Review on YouTube*
*(https://www.youtube.com/user/JoczProductions/playlists)*


• *Fiveable's AP U.S. History study resources (https://fiveable.me/ap-us-history)*

Made in the USA
Las Vegas, NV
28 September 2023